P9-EMG-131

Digging Up America

Books by Frank C. Hibben

THE LOST AMERICANS

HUNTING AMERICAN LIONS

HUNTING AMERICAN BEARS

PREHISTORIC MAN IN EUROPE

FRANK C. HIBBEN

Digging Up America

 HILL AND WANG • NEW YORK

Library of Congress Catalog Card Number: 60-10518

First Edition

Manufactured in the United States of America
by American Book–Stratford Press

Contents

ACKNOWLEDGMENTS

For the photographs reproduced here by permission, the author expresses thanks to the American Museum of Natural History for photographs, plate numbers 7-16, 19, 24-26, 28-46; to the Colorado Museum of Natural History for photograph, plate number 1; and to the Denver Museum of Natural History for photograph, plate number 5.

Illustrations

Digging Up America

1

American Beginnings

THE HUMAN MAMMAL is the only one of all of the primates to possess tools and other material artifacts. Man is the only living creature which has developed a true society. Human beings alone have come to recognize a Supreme Being and to worship him in different forms of religion, and only man has developed language by which he can pass on his experiences to the next generation.

The material and mental accomplishments of man are a result of his being created in a marvelous form. What distinguishes man significantly from the lower apes is his complex brain. Its surface and divisions are larger and more complicated than those of the brain of any other living thing. It is from this brain that the cultural superiority of man derived. Human beings, during the course of their evolution, rose erect on their hind feet. Their backbones became S-shaped, while the backs of most primitive four-footed animals retain the arcuate form. The erect posture freed their forelimbs for development into hands. Even the great apes still use their hands in a crutchlike way when walking. Man can use his hands to make and use tools.

With his hands and superior brain, man emerged as the most powerful creature on earth. The original development of man took place in Asia, Africa, and Europe. Where, then, did the American story begin? And how?

The story of American archaeology begins at the end, not at the beginning. The most recent clues, the latest cultures, are those that we know the most about. In America, as everywhere else that man has left his traces, the story of a few centuries ago is fairly clear. However, when we go back several thousand years, the picture is less clear. The very earliest beginnings, perhaps, are obscured forever. The archaeologist, like the sleuth in a good detective story, unscrambles the conflicting clues and assembles all his facts in chronological order and tells the story of ancient times from the beginning to the end. Although the archaeologist digs from the top down, he tells the story from the bottom up.

A century ago, there was no such thing as American archaeology. At least, archaeology or anthropology would have been difficult to find in books or in college curricula. The study of antiquity had already begun in a modest way in Europe. Crude flint tools had been identified as part of the first culture left behind by ancient men in France. But when similar flint tools were eagerly sought on the plains of North America and in the valleys of Mexico, none could be found. It is true that early investigators in America found stone lance points, fragments of pottery, and the foundations of buildings, but these did not seem to be as old as the European ones, or as significant. Gradually, as anthropologists studied all of the works of men, both ancient and modern, the picture became clearer. At first the investigators thought that the evidence of the beginnings of man might be hidden beneath the mold of some American forest or river valley. Today we know that this is not so. Man definitely originated in the Old World—that is, in Europe, Africa, and Asia.

The first European archaeologists were impeded in their work by the prevailing religious thought of a century ago. For example, adherence to the Calvinistic interpretation of creation, which allowed only about 6,000 years for the creation, and civilized development of man, prevented many Europeans from accepting the fact that flint tools and the bones of Ice Age animals found in Europe were evidence of human life going back many thousands of years. Thus in 1850 when Boucher de Perthes, a French tax collector, found rough, chipped "fist axes" deeply buried in glacial gravels in northern France, most of the scientists of the day refused to believe the evidence they saw before them. It was almost fifty years before European scholars generally accepted the fact that the first human beings had been in the Old World about one million years ago during the first part of the last glacial period.

Inevitably, the early archaeological studies in the Americas were based upon European ideas, although, perhaps because of the greater religious freedom in the New World, the first American archaeologists were not so limited by strict religious interpretations. At first, though, the work of New World scientists both in North and South America was obstructed by the same difficulties that hampered the railroads, the mining men, and the pioneers themselves. Whereas Europe had been populated and civilized for thousands of years, the New World was virgin wilderness. At the time when Boucher de Perthes in France was demonstrating that the flint fist axes he had found there were actually the tools of extremely ancient Europeans, Americans were pushing across the Santa Fe Trail and the California gold rush was in progress. At this same time South America was being explored and the jungles of the Amazon were just being penetrated. In any part of the world, exploration and exploitation come first. It is only later that men begin to look into their past.

Another thing that discouraged early American efforts was the initial disappointment connected with the discovery that human beings did not originate in North or South America. This fact, of course, was not known all at once, or even conceded by some until the beginning of the twentieth century. As late as the 1890s, no less a person than Dr. W. H. Holmes, later chief of the Bureau of American Ethnology of the Smithsonian Institution, was still searching for the remains of Ice Age man in New Jersey, Pennsylvania, and Virginia. Other American scientists, especially in New England where modern civilization has left its heaviest imprint, were looking for fossils of men and ancient tools like those which were being discovered in Europe and in Asia.

Even before the period of exploration in North and South America was over, scientists were looking for the bones or the tools of ape men. And some discoveries were made. In 1835 a Danish explorer named Lund discovered human skeletons in some caves near a lake called Lagoa Santa in southeastern Brazil. These skeletons and the bones of many kinds of Ice Age animals were buried in the mud of the caves in such a way that Lund thought the human remains to be those of extremely ancient men. At the time of this discovery over a century ago, most of the ape men of Europe, Africa, and Asia had not yet been found. Therefore, Lund was not disappointed when the Lagoa

Santa skeletons were not primitive in appearance. The Lagoa Santa skulls do not differ radically from the bony skulls of modern Brazilian Indians.

It was not until 1956 that an expedition from the W. H. Over Museum at the University of South Dakota dug again at Lagoa Santa and demonstrated that the skeletons there which had caused so much controversy were not so ancient after all. We now know through the work of Dr. Wesley Hurt that the Lagoa Santa skeletons were those of South American Indians of only the last few hundred years. These "corpora delecti" were interred in the caves of Lagoa Santa when water levels rose and fell with the wet and dry seasons.

There were other finds in North and South America. In 1846 a physician, Dr. M. Dickeson, found a human pelvis deeply buried in the clay and detritus near the city of Natchez, Mississippi. This was at first widely heralded as "Natchez man." However, more than a hundred years later, in 1954, a careful scientist, Dr. George Quimby, concluded that Natchez man was probably a comparatively modern American Indian who had drowned in a flash flood long ago, but he was not sure. Even today, fossil bones and teeth of Ice Age animals are being found in the clay near where the Natchez skeleton was discovered.

As each allegedly ancient skeleton was disqualified for a place in antiquity, the evidence of early American tools also proved disappointing. Crude, chopperlike hand axes found in New England by eager American scientists were at first thought to be the tools of Ice Age Americans. As the story of European prehistory began to unfold, American professors and the first American archaeologists thought that they had evidence of a similar story on the American side of the Atlantic. It was a crushing disappointment for them to learn that these American fist axes and choppers were the crude implements of comparatively late American Indians. In some cases the tools were rejects which American Indian workmen had started poorly and then thrown away in disgust. American archaeologists learned the hard way that a crude implement is not necessarily an early one in the human story.

A typical find was one made on the Abbott farm near Trenton, New Jersey. The first discovery was made there in 1873 around the time of the most startling archaeological revelations in Europe. A "Trenton man" was later postulated as being typical of the earliest American and comparable with any of the prehistoric men of Java or even with the famous Neanderthal man who was discovered in a cave in the gorge of Neanderthal, near Düsseldorf, Germany, in 1856. Discussions of Trenton man and his antiquity fill the scientific journals of the antiquarian societies of the early 1900s. It was not until the time of the First World War that it was conclusively demonstrated by further digging that the early men who lived near Trenton, New Jersey, were American Indians of a much later era than the fossil types in Africa, Asia, and Europe.

In 1891, Dr. Eugene Dubois, a Dutch surgeon, found the primitive apelike skull and the thigh bone of *Pithecanthropus erectus* in river gravels on the island of Java. American scientists were present when Dr. Dubois displayed his fabulous find at scientific meetings. The name which Dr. Dubois gave to this now extinct creature means "ape man who walked erect."

But slowly and inexorably, as North and South America were more carefully explored, the evidence mounted that human beings did not evolve on these shores. The first Americans were not primitive ape men, and the Garden of Eden is not to be found in the valley of the Mississippi or the Amazon. It became abundantly clear during the first decades of the twentieth century that man did not originate in the Americas.

Somehow human beings had entered North and South America in the middle of the story of man. The exact date of their arrival could only be guessed at. In the 1920s it was thought that human beings were on American shores only a few centuries before the birth of Christ at the very earliest. Even so, the American archaeologists of three and four decades ago were goaded into increasing activity. They tried to push back the antiquity of the human occupation of the New World as far as possible. As the certainty grew that man and his culture did not originate in America, it was necessary to answer other pressing questions. When did humans first come here, and how?

2

How Old Is America?

AMERICAN ARCHAEOLOGY and archaeologists forged ahead during the twenties. There was much to discover. American archaeologists had to answer several crucial questions before New World backgrounds could be outlined even in vague terms.

Their activity took two forms. The first of these was actual digging. The second was the development of scientific methods of analyzing what had been dug. Scientific activity in both these fields reached a peak in America in the twenties. It is no accident that the majority of new archaeological time-telling techniques were discovered in the United States.

Egyptologists and those interested in the backgrounds of Mesopotamia and Greece also excavated during this time. Indeed, many of the excavators were Americans who felt that they could best discover the most important remains of antiquity in the Old World. But even the great expeditions of Dr. James Breasted in Egypt and Mesopotamia or the American schools of archaeology in Greece and Rome could not equal in scope the activity of some hundreds of American archaeologists digging in the Andean, Mexican, and Mayan ruins, in the American Southwest, or in the Mound Builder area east of the Mississippi. Universities, endowed institutions, and private persons explored and dug. This splurge of activity is still going on and it has produced rich results.

Perhaps the most pressing question which the American archaeologists sought to answer was: How old? By "How old?" is meant, of course, "How long ago was America first inhabited by human beings?"

A logical source of an answer to this question seemed to be those places where civilizations had reached great cultural levels in the past, since it seemed probable that such civilizations were the oldest. Old World archaeologists had worked on this premise for many years. Also, it was hoped that the earliest Americans might have left records like those found in the Old World and especially in Egypt. The Egyptians had kept careful records of the succession of their kings. A late Egyptian priest had divided all the kings or pharaohs into groups of families called dynasties, and their succession was also carefully recorded. The Egyptians also evolved a calendar, at first based upon the movement of Sirius, the Dog Star, which they called Soth. The Egyptians also recorded a solar year and on this basis evolved a calendar so exact that the Romans later copied the system and it has become the basis of the calendar which we use today.

One of the most impressive civilizations in America was the Mayan, and archaeologists turned to the Mayan ruins hoping to come upon records which would enable them to discover just when Mayan civilization began. They found that the Mayas had developed a complex calendar but, for reasons which will be discussed in a later chapter, the studies which the archaeologists were able to make proved disappointing and inconclusive.

Since the Mayan calendar could not tell exactly how old American culture might be, the archaeologists turned to other places and other methods. In the American Southwest, archaeologists had found rich evidences of developed civilizations. These civilizations, like those in Mexico and Central America, were based upon agriculture. Unlike the people of Central America, however, the early southwesterners had not developed glyph symbols or calendric notations. If the ancient southwestern Americans kept track of time by year counts or some such simple notation, they made these year counts on perishable materials so that they have been lost forever.

Archaeologists have an almost universal method for telling time. This is stratigraphy. If one layer of cultural material is on top of another, then the lowermost is the earlier and the upper is the later. If there is a sequence of superimposed cultural layers, the archaeologist can postulate a whole sequence of cultures in that order. Two Danish archaeologists had worked out the science of stratigraphy in their native Denmark over a century before the Americans used the system in the American Southwest. The science of stratigraphy is simple, straightforward, and almost foolproof.

It was stratigraphy that Dr. A. V. Kidder used in the 1920s when he began to dig at the ruin of Pecos Pueblo near Pecos, New Mexico. Dr. Kidder was one of the many archaeologists who came to the American Southwest to try to discover the cultural history of the many pueblo ruins, forts, pit houses, and plazas of New Mexico and

Arizona. At the time Dr. Kidder and his fellow archaeologists began their excavations, the Pecos Pueblo ruins were as mysterious as the Mayan. No one could tell whether they were thousands of years old, or only a few hundred.

Dr. Kidder began to dig at Pecos Pueblo because it was one of the few pueblo cities which had extended into historic times. When Coronado, the Spanish conquistador, had marched up the Rio Grande in 1540, Pecos was still a living town. During the time that New Mexico was a Spanish province, the pueblo of Pecos was mentioned by several Spanish governors. It was not until 1838 that Pecos was finally abandoned under the onslaughts of attacking Apaches and Comanches.

Dr. Kidder began digging the ruin of Pecos from a known level dated in the first third of the nineteenth century, and thence back through successive levels of culture into earlier and earlier southwestern times. Dr. Kidder and his associates were able to determine relative time and closely approximate the actual history of the American Southwest in terms of years. Stratigraphy was helpful in determining dates for the pueblo of Pecos but its usefulness was limited by two major difficulties. The first of these was that there were gaps in the stratigraphic story. The second and almost insurmountable difficulty was that at no place in the American Southwest where archaeologists had dug were all of the cultural levels piled one on top of another.

Archaeologists, working at other sites in the Southwest, began to discover evidences of cultures which were obviously earlier than those at the earliest levels of Pecos. Archaeologists working in southern Arizona found indications of farming peoples who seemed to have nothing to do with the type of pueblo life found at the Pecos ruin. Through study of the different kinds of pottery, masonry, and tools which the Pecos Pueblo Indians made, archaeologists were able to relate their findings to other pueblo ruins where similar artifacts were discovered. Nevertheless, stratigraphy could not show how long the various periods of early Pecos had endured. The depth of refuse and tumbled walls of a ruined town cannot be measured in terms of years.

This problem was solved in a most ingenious way by the use of the tree-ring calendar which was discovered by an astronomer working in the American Southwest. This scientist, Dr. A. E. Douglass, was studying sunspots in Arizona and, in connection with his studies, examined the growth rings of trees as revealed in a cross section of the trunk. He wanted to see if cycles of sunspot activity had affected the climate and consequently the growth of trees in times past. First he examined the cross sections of large yellow pines as cut by modern lumber mills. Dr. Douglass found that the growth rings of the pine trees reflected the climate of the past very faithfully and especially the wet and dry seasons. Since some of the trees were several centuries old, this record could be carried back for hundreds of years.

In order to carry this record even further back than the life span of a single tree, Dr. Douglass and his associates procured wood specimens from the roof beams of the Hopi Indian pueblos of northern Arizona. One of the Hopi towns, Oraibi, had been continuously occupied since the coming of the Spaniards in 1540. After placating the modern Hopis with a gift of purple velvet in compensation for boring holes in the beams of their houses, Dr. Douglass extracted a series of specimens which carried his tree-ring calendar further into the past. By supplementing the series by wood from the ruins of even earlier Hopi towns in the same area, the tree-ring dates were pushed further back into antiquity. On June 22, 1929, Dr. Douglass found a single piece of wood whose rings bridged a gap and the calendar was complete. In this accidental way, Dr. Douglass discovered a calendar which could be used to date exactly archaeological ruins which contained pieces of wood. In the arid Southwest, logs and roof beams are quite often preserved even in buildings of very early date. This tree-ring calendar promised to answer the questions of chronology in early America.

By use of this tree-ring calendar, the early levels of Pecos Pueblo were finally dated and most of the other ruins of the American Southwest also yielded their time secrets to the tree-ring experts or "dendrochronologists" as they were called. By overlapping older and still older fragments of wood from various archaeological sites, a master chart of dendrochronology pushed further and further back into antiquity. Pieces of sensitive wood with their telltale wide and narrow rings formed a master chart complete back to the year 11 A.D. Dr. Douglass himself, who had inadvertently discovered dendrochronology, carried this master chart in his head. Given a piece of wood from an ancient ruin, he was able to move it up and down the master chart until the rings fitted exactly. Dr. Douglass called the outside ring of the unknown specimen "the cutting date." This was the year at which some stone axe of long ago had chopped down the sapling that became a part of some early building.

Through dendrochronology, the dates of the various peoples in the Southwest were as precise as though the successive tribes had left an exact calendric account of their history.

But dendrochronology did not solve all of the problems of the American archaeologist. The beginnings of the American story were still unknown since wood from the earliest times had not been preserved in significant quantities. Also, when dendrochronology was used in other areas of America, it worked indifferently or not at all. In the eastern section of the United States, for example, tree-ring counts proved very unsatisfactory. And in the comparatively well-watered Mississippi Valley, trees, both ancient and modern, showed little variation in their ring patterns, so little, in fact, that the scientists could not see exactly the patterns of wet and dry years. Even in the Southwest where the tree-ring calendar had been evolved, it was discovered that different kinds of wood would not work equally well. Pine, fir, and piñon trees usually yielded a date if the outside or bark ring of the piece of wood was preserved. But other kinds of trees were also used by ancient builders. These other species were difficult or impossible to use for tree-ring dating purposes. Also, as the rainfall varied in ancient times from place to place in the Southwest, it was necessary to draw up a different master chart for different districts. The master chart which Dr. Douglass had worked out for parts of Arizona would not work in the valley of the Rio Grande.

The man who discovered the most important clues to the story of the first Americans was even further removed from archaeology than Dr. Douglass. This man, George McJunkin by name, was a bronco-riding Negro cowboy on the old Shoemaker ranch in northeastern New Mexico. McJunkin, a good cowboy, occasionally expressed interest in the Apache Indian flint points which he found on the ranch. Although he was no archaeologist, George McJunkin had a keen curiosity. It was this curiosity that led to the accidental discovery of human beginnings in America.

In the spring of 1926, while George McJunkin was following the trail of some straying cows along the bank of a deep arroyo known locally as Dead Horse Gulch, he noticed some whitened bones sticking from the mud of the opposite side of the arroyo. The bones were about the size of cow bones, but they were buried twenty feet below the surface. This circumstance piqued his curiosity, so he climbed off his horse and slid down the side of the gulch. He took out his cattle knife and pried with its blade among the whitened bones. He found a flint point which he judged to be an arrowhead made by some ancient Indian hunter. The flint point was unique as it had a groove or flute which channeled each face and was not notched like ordinary Indian arrowheads. But why, he reasoned, should the animal bones and the flint point which had killed the animal be buried so deeply?

This also seemed strange to the people to whom the cowboy told the story of the buried bones. A local citizen, a banker of Raton, New Mexico, brought the find to the attention of Dr. J. D. Figgins of Colorado.

Dr. Figgins was a paleontologist. He was only casually interested in the fact that man-made flint points had been discovered with the bones. He was most interested in the bones themselves. Dr. Figgins thought that these bones might be a part of the carcass of some early and now extinct kind of animal, and he was quite right.

When Dr. Figgins excavated in Dead Horse Gulch, he found that the bones buried there belonged to a kind of bison typical of the last of the Ice Age in North America. Dr. Figgins named the bison *Bison taylori,* in honor of Dr. E. Taylor who was then head of the Colorado Museum. He further deduced that no *Bison taylori* had lived in what is now New Mexico for 10,000 years. The flint points found among the bones of these Ice Age bison were indisputable evidence that human beings had also been there during the Ice Age.

American archaeologists came from all parts of the continent to look at George McJunkin's discovery. More excavations were carried out and the skeletons of additional *Bison taylori* laid bare. And between the ribs of several of these were the same curious flint points which George McJunkin had found. Because of the nearness of Dead Horse Gulch to the small town of Folsom, New Mexico, the men who had killed these bison were labeled "Folsom men" and the characteristically shaped points which they had left behind were named "Folsom points." No human remains were included in the original Folsom discovery. The bison carcasses at the Folsom site did not seem to mark a regular camping place of these early Americans or a spot where they had lived. Rather, they seemed to be evidence of a single hunt. Probably a herd of some 30 bison had been drinking at a small pond or a lake where none exists today. The Folsom men had sprung out of ambush and killed the animals on the spot, and then cut up a few of the carcasses and hauled the meat away.

The importance of the discovery was obvious. In this one find, the history of early America had been rolled back 10,000 years or more. Dr. Figgins did not employ the methods of tree-ring dating or even stratigraphy. He based his deductions on the association of human evidences with animal bones of a known geological period. This type of time fixing had been done extensively in Europe. The flint fist axes found by Boucher de Perthes in northern Europe had been dated largely by means of the animal bones of extinct types found with the tools.

The Folsom find touched off a whole series of discoveries relating to Ice Age times in the New World. The curious Folsom points were not arrowheads, as George McJunkin had first thought. Characterized by shallow grooves running up their faces, the points were used on throwing lances or light spears; they were lethal weapons. Fluted Folsom points began to turn up over a wide area. They were revealed in places where arroyos had cut down through Ice Age soil levels, or in spots where the drought winds of the 1930s had scoured away the soil's surface. Camping places of Folsom men turned up in eastern New Mexico, eastern Colorado, and the panhandle of Texas.

Now archaeologists painstakingly collected all of the clues of Ice Age Americans. Soon they were able to recognize a number of variations of Folsom man. These different groups were usually distinguishable by different kinds of lance points. At Plainview, Texas, a Plainview man was described by means of the lance points he made. A Clovis man was named from a great camping site at Clovis, New Mexico. A Yuma type received its name from Yuma County, Colorado, where points of a still different variety were first found. Some of these early hunting Americans habitually killed *Bison taylori*. Clovis man specialized in hunting the mammoth, also typical of Ice Age America. The Yuma hunters killed a later type of bison almost like our modern "buffalo." Thus, by careful examination of Ice Age deposits, and by means of the animal bones found in them, archaeologists began to outline the earliest history of the New World.

One of the most significant additions to the fascinating picture of Ice Age beginnings was made when a student named Ken Davis discovered a cave near Albuquerque, New Mexico. Called the Sandia Cave, it was excavated in 1938 by archaeologists from the University of New Mexico after they found, inside the cave, bones of extinct Ice Age animals and implements made by man. Grubbing in the suffocating dust of the now dry cavern, the archaeologists found two ancient cave floors littered with human debris. Both floors were marked by fire pits and the scattered and cracked bones of bison, elephants, horses, and camels. On the floor of the upper cave were found a few of the typical fluted points of the Folsom hunters. On the lower level the archaeologists found lance points of a different form. These were shouldered on one end to facilitate hafting and were more crudely chipped. These latter points were called Sandia points.

By using stratigraphy and reckoning from the indications of the wet and dry periods of Sandia Cave, Professor Kirk Bryan of Harvard University, who did the geological work, was able to deduce that the Sandia hunters had lived there some 25,000 years before and had cooked the meat of now extinct animals.

Archaeologists working on the problem of Ice Age man in America were disappointed not to find any human skeletons on the littered camp sites or in the cave where these early hunters had lived. Animal bones were there in plenty. Paleontologists assisting the archaeologists were able to identify different kinds of bison, elephants, and horses. These animals were found with the different sorts of lance points and other flint tools which distinguished different tribes or groups of early American hunters. Historical gaps began to be filled in with further digging and more archaeological finds.

The hiatus between the early Ice Age Americans and the later agricultural peoples began to be spotted with discoveries to make an almost continuous series. There were also finds which did not seem to fit into the larger picture. Dr. George Carter, a professor from Johns Hopkins University, found some crude implements in Ice Age gravels near San Diego, California, in 1951. These roughly made tools were buried in levels which indicated that they belonged to a time before that of the Sandia hunters. The crudity of the implements indicated the possibility that there had been a true paleolithic era in the early history of California. However, some American archaeologists thought that Dr. Carter's finds were not implements at all but merely stone chipped by frost action and the natural movement of the earth.

But whatever the exact beginnings of humanity in America, there was no doubt that some kind of man had been on these shores during the last part of the Ice Age. The dating of these times by the associated bones of extinct animals was far from exact. For one thing, the time of extinction of the elephants and other Ice Age animals is known only in a general way. Archaeologists were in the position of the New Mexican rancher who found on his ranch the skeleton of a mammoth with a lance point embedded within the bones. "You can tell," he remarked, "that the fellows who threw that spear were here an awful long time ago."

Geologists who had been called in by archaeologists to help them with their dating troubles began to refine their techniques. Normally geologists do not try to pinpoint dates in the past. A geologist is chiefly concerned with the story of the earth itself. Geologists now figure that the earth has been in approximately its present form about 1,832 million years. It is no wonder that geologists had such difficulty in trying to adapt themselves to mere millennia and infinitesimal centuries. But they tried.

With painstaking effort they began to develop a timetable of the Ice Age, which took place just before modern times. The Ice Age is called by geologists the "Pleistocene." It lasted about one million years. During this period, great masses of glacial ice formed on top of the continents in the Northern Hemisphere. Parts of the Southern Hemisphere had at the same time been affected by pluviations, or rainy periods. In North America, Europe, and northern

Asia, glacial ice had formed four times during the Pleistocene and four times had melted away. These four glaciations were the reflection of major changes in climate and rainfall in the Northern Hemisphere. The climatic changes and the gathering and waning of ice masses profoundly affected all life around the edges of the glacial centers.

Different kinds of animals lived during the interglacial periods. Loving warmth, these animals contrasted sharply with the different species of arctic and cold-loving varieties which were present when the ice sheets covered great sections of Europe, Asia, and North America. Human remains found with the different kinds of animals could be dated in this way. The geologist was able to tell the archaeologist that a camp site littered with the bones of the woolly rhinoceros had been used by men during the time of the fourth glacial advance in Europe. Human tools were found with the characteristic bones of the hippopotamus, indicating that human beings had lived there during a warm interglacial period. However, the time of these glacial and interglacial periods remained vague—at best, geologists spoke of tens of thousands of years—but the sequence was correct. To remove some of the vagueness, they worked out several fascinating techniques to try to pinpoint archaeological time.

One of the most interesting of these was based on a principle like that of the tree-ring calendar, but used varves, or layers of silt, formed of gravel and mud. A varve is usually laid down in a glacial lake by the deposition of material carried by a river. During a warm glacial summer of ancient times, the rivers, swollen by melted ice, deposited gravel and pebbles on the bed of an ancient lake. During the subsequent winter period, the volume of the river was shrunken by freezing. The fine mud sediment which it carried was deposited in a thin coating over the coarse gravel of the previous summer. A varve is such a deposit of coarse and fine sediment and each one is the record of an actual year.

Series of thousands of varves were identified as records of the same thousands of years of glacial time at the edges of the glaciers in Europe. Similar varve counts were made in New York State and in other places in North America where glacial rivers had existed. As the varve counts were numbered in actual years, archaeologists eagerly seized upon the resultant glacial calendar to date human happenings exactly.

Unfortunately, the varve calendar was of little help. Human remains were seldom, if ever, found in or near the varves. And it was also impossible to tell exactly when such sediments were first laid down and when the series ended.

Another method of dating was to study the kinds of trees and bushes which had grown around the edges of the ice masses during glacial times. But since wood and leaves are perishable, scientists could not hope to find sufficient evidence of ancient vegetation to make accurate studies.

Then a Danish scientist made a curious discovery in bogs and swamps left behind by the melting of the last glaciation in northern Europe. He found that in the black muck of these swamps where little oxygen entered, the pollen of ancient plants was remarkably well preserved. A piece of mud pulled up from the bottom of one such swamp could be stained by chemicals to make the pollen grains visible. Under the microscope, each pollen grain was not only apparent but its species could be identified.

But the use of pollen grains in compiling a timetable also proved impossible since the method was applicable in Europe only for the last or fourth glaciation and chiefly during its waning stages. Pollen studies in the New England states, Colorado, and other places in the New World were of limited usefulness. The pollen timetable (or "hay fever chart," as it was humorously referred to by some archaeologists) helped some in the dating of human happenings at the very end of the Pleistocene Period. Before that, the record was spotty and inconclusive.

Other geological methods were attempted to help the archaeologists pinpoint the earliest history of the Americas. Geological studies of river terraces were of some use. The terraces formed along the banks of rivers are the result of the ebb and flow of the same rivers during different glacial times. When the rivers are in flood from melting ice, the increased volume of water tends to scour and cut the banks. During cold periods, the diminished volume of water tends to deposit the sand and gravel it carries. Early Americans often lived on the banks of these rivers. Geologists are sometimes able to date different river terraces and the human camp sites found upon them. Unfortunately these dates are usually given in relative terms or, at best, in vague approximations of glacial time.

Professor Kirk Bryan, the same Harvard geologist who worked on the Sandia Cave, also made a classic geological study of a camp site of Folsom man in eastern Colorado in 1940. This place was called the Lindenmeier site, from the name of the ranch on which it is situated. Professor Bryan and his associates were able to distinguish a series of glacial happenings which were evidenced by beds of gravel, layers of silt, and the cutting and filling in of arroyos.

The last major glacial period in North America is called the Wisconsin Period, because the first major evidences of glaciation were identified in that state. During the Wisconsin Period, most of the Rocky Mountains were covered by an ice cap. The Lindenmeier site had probably been chosen as the camping place of Folsom men because it stood at the edge of the icy cliffs. The place was cold and drafty, but it was handy to water and to the herds of Ice Age bison which fed on the grasslands not far away.

Professor Bryan and his band of geologists found that the last part of the Wisconsin Period, during which the hunters had lived in what is now the state of Wisconsin, was not a simple period at all. There were a number of fluctuations in the melting of the Wisconsin ice. The forces which had originally caused the ice to form apparently reversed themselves several times. These minor oscillations or fluctuations of the Wisconsin ice were reflected in corresponding wet and dry, and warm and cool periods in the surrounding country. The geologists were able to fit the human happenings, as evidenced by the stone tools and the bones of slaughtered animals, into the geological timetable which they discovered. This helped tremendously in the dating of the first Americans. Each camp site, each place where early American hunters had made a kill, could be fitted into the scheme. Geologists even timidly dated some of these happenings, but usually in terms of millennia.

Even with refinements of geological technique, it was obvious that the question, "How old?" had not yet been answered. Geological changes on the face of the earth are so slow that human happenings can scarcely be fitted into them with chronological exactitude. In the eyes of man, the hills are eternal. To a geologist, the hills are nothing of the sort, since they can be scoured away by a continental glacier in only a few tens of thousands of years. By studying extinct animals and glacial changes, and by using climatic charts, archaeologists now knew that human beings had been in the New World for 25,000 years or thereabouts. It remained for other sciences to develop methods applicable for dating the first Americans precisely.

3

Radioactive Time

❦

Archaeologists continued to call upon other sciences in trying to date early human evidences. Chemistry was one of them. Many flint tools are covered on their surfaces by a thin layer of "patina." Flint, or flinty kinds of stone, acquire a patina over a long period of time and more especially by being buried in the earth. Patination is an actual chemical change in the surface of the stone, brought about by surrounding soil acids in the earth in which the flint is buried. Flintlike stones were the favorite material from which early man fashioned his implements, and so it seemed that they would be useful in determining dates. If the chemists could work out a timetable of patination, archaeologists might be able to determine the exact age of the patinated implements which they found.

In the 1920s, a number of chemists worked on this problem for a long time. The idea did not work as an archaeological timetable, for the rate of patination of flint was erratic. One Sandia point might be patinated heavily, and another point only a few feet away and in the same level have no patination whatsoever. Reluctantly, archaeologists and chemists abandoned this scheme.

Not at all discouraged, some ingenious archaeologists devised another method of dating finds. They had discovered particles of a mineral called magnetite in many archaeological deposits. Magnetite particles are usually long needle-like crystals of very small size. The crystals work like tiny magnets, having north and south poles. In running water or in thin mud, the particles of magnetite orient themselves along the lines of magnetic force across the face of the earth.

We know that the magnetic poles of the earth do not remain constant. Magnetic north moves from year to year, all around the North Pole, in some cases several degrees away from true north. The deviation of magnetic north is well known and is plotted on most charts by years. A notation such as "Each year after 1960, add 2°" shows the amount and direction that the magnetic pole moves in a given period in a certain area. Magnetite particles of a particular year will align themselves according to the magnetic north of that time. Then, if the mud or wet sand in which they are embedded dries out or is made into an adobe brick or plastered into an ancient floor, their original alignment will remain.

An archaeologist wishing to date his diggings by "fossil magnetism" could take out a sample of sand after carefully orienting it before removal. Examination of the magnetite particles in the sample would indicate where the magnetic poles of the earth had been at the time the sand was fluid. This would be the year when that piece of earth was on the surface of a human camp and was washed by the rains and snows of that time. Later, when it was buried by human debris, the magnetite particles would become fixed and the record of their magnetic direction cemented in place.

Fossil magnetism did not solve all the problems of the archaeologist or answer exactly the question, "How old?" In many sites there are no magnetite particles. Even in places where there are, the little magnetite compasses do not always point in a constant direction.

During and after World War II, archaeologists turned for help to the science of atomic fission. Dr. Willard Libby, a physicist working with a radioactive material, made a discovery which proved useful. Dr. Libby had been interested in two major aspects of the new science of radiochemistry since before World War II. He was studying natural radioactivity in the lighter chemical elements and also was seeking methods for measuring extremely weak radioactive substances. The invention of a device called the "screen wall counter" was announced in 1933, long before the first atomic bomb was produced.

All radioactive substances, whether very radioactive or only mildly so, bombard their surroundings with small particles or rays. These particles have been named by scientists after the Greek letters alpha, beta, and gamma. Alpha, beta, and gamma rays fly off from a piece of radioactive material like sky rockets from a crate of exploding fireworks. Violently radioactive materials such as pitchblende throw off so many of these rays at such a lively rate that the bombardment is easily detected by a machine such as a Geiger counter. However, some light chemical elements throw off radioactive rays in such a scattered and mild pattern that they are difficult to detect. The screen wall counter was a device which recorded the presence of such flying particles and made it possible to count them as they struck the counter.

All this would seem to lie purely in the realm of physics and chemistry. Archaeologists certainly would never have heard of the screen wall counter or alpha, beta, or gamma rays had it not been for Dr. Libby's interest in certain types of natural radioactivity. Research which he did during the war years and into the late 1940s led Dr. Libby to believe that certain mildly radioactive substances were formed in the upper atmosphere by the action of cosmic rays. Two of these substances were identified as tritium, and a form of carbon called "carbon 14." Dr. Libby particularly concentrated his attention on carbon 14, which is a very faintly radioactive form of carbon. Carbon 14 is constantly being formed in the upper atmosphere by the action of cosmic rays, and there is a never-ending supply of it in the air. Researchers, working with Dr. Libby, found that it is present in all living matter. Every kind of plant and animal absorbs carbon 14 from its surroundings.

There is a slight amount of radioactivity almost everywhere. The Geiger counter of a man prospecting for uranium ore often picks up this faint radioactivity from trees, and even from the air itself. This general radioactivity is often called "background" activity and must be taken into account in any search for alpha, beta, or gamma ray activity.

An atomic calendar was based upon the fact that the carbon 14 in all living things disintegrates at a fixed rate. All radioactive substances tend to disintegrate as they throw off particles of themselves in alpha, beta, and gamma rays. This disintegration phenomenon resembles a kettle of water boiling dry, with the boiling process comparable to the radioactivity. The only difference is that most radioactive materials disintegrate only after a very long period of time—in most cases, thousands of years. This disintegration of substances is measured in what is called "half life." The half life of a pound of carbon 14 will, by radioactivity, be reduced to half a pound in 5,568 years. This half pound will, by the continuous process of throwing off rays, be reduced to one quarter pound in another 5,568 years. As the process continues, the weight of the substance is cut in half with each half-life period. The substance remains carbon 14, however, and it still disintegrates at a fixed rate.

It can immediately be seen how important it was for scientists working on this fascinating problem to evolve some sort of counting device which would exactly measure the amount of carbon 14 in a given sample. The count could be made with relatively small error in the laboratory, and the exact concentration of carbon 14 in a piece of wood, an animal tooth, or a fragment of burned bone could be determined. The scientists had two newly discovered facts with which to work. The first of these was that carbon 14 was formed at a constant rate in the atmosphere and was absorbed by all plants and animals from the air. The second was that carbon 14 disintegrates at a fixed rate with a measurable half life of 5,568 years. This process continues as long as the animal or plant *is alive.* The moment a tree is cut down, the instant an animal is killed, the inert body ceases to take in carbon 14. However, the radioactive carbon 14 already in the trunk of the tree or in the body of the elephant continues to disintegrate at the same mathematically fixed rate.

Dr. Libby and his associates found that they could measure the amount of carbon in the body of anything which had once been alive no matter where in the world the thing had lived. By their laboratory methods they were able to tell the exact instant at which a flint spear had ended the life of some Ice Age elephant or a stone axe had cut down a tree.

To check their system, scientists measured the amount of carbon 14 in wood from mummy cases in which pharaohs of ancient Egypt had ben buried. These pharaohs were listed on the ancient Egyptian king lists and the time of their death is known in terms of our present calendar. Carbon 14 dates derived from Egyptian samples and the dates at which the kings were known to have been buried coincided very closely. In 1949 it was announced that carbon 14 could be used for an archaeological calendar.

Archaeologists were jubilant. Here was a time scale evolved and perfected by chemists and physicists. Its calculations were mathematical and not subject to guesswork. The archaeologists felt that their science had come of age in the atomic period. No longer was it necessary to deal vaguely with millennia and centuries. Happenings of many thousands of years ago could be dated with as much certainty as the written history of modern times.

In the first flush of enthusiasm following the announcement of carbon 14 dating, archaeologists felt justified in regarding the radioactive calendar as the method for solving all their chronological problems everywhere. True, Dr. Libby and his associates found that approximately 25,000 years was the practical limit of the new calendar. Beyond this period, the amount of carbon 14 in any given substance is so slight as to be most difficult to measure. However, archaeologists pointed out that if we could tell the story of the last 25,000 years exactly, most of the archaeological mysteries of the world could be solved. Certainly 25,000 years would include most, if not all, of the antiquity of the New World.

Immediately following the development of the carbon 14 calendar, a number of significant dates were announced. These were based on studies of fragments of charcoal, corncobs, charred bone, and other once-living substances. The specimens were gathered from North and South America, Egypt, Manchuria, and Europe. Because of the difficulty of measuring the amount of carbon 14 in the samples, these dates were subject to errors of about 1,000 years. Laboratory scientists realized that their counting devices were inadequate for the exact determination of the number of particles emanating from a given piece of matter.

However, even this major defect of the radioactive calendar was largely corrected by improvement in laboratory methods. Laboratory technicians soon developed a method of turning the sample to be dated into a gas. In gaseous form, the emanations of the various particles could be counted much more easily. During the late 1950s, as more and more dates were published, the error which had to be included with the date grew less and less. In many of the samples, the error could be reduced to 30 years or less, and this is certainly exact when we are dealing with earliest prehistory.

There were other limitations to writing ancient history with carbon 14 dates. It was found that certain things, even though parts of once living bodies, did not have enough carbon 14 within them to be measured. For example, not enough carbon 14 is deposited in the walls of the bones of animals to activate sensitive laboratory instruments. And yet bones are the major archaeological evidence yielded by ancient camp sites and places where human beings once lived. Curiously enough, burned bones yield to investigation because the charring of the bone fixes carbon 14 derived from the air. If some ancient fellow dropped the leg bone of an Ice Age horse onto his campfire, the charred remains of the bone can be dated very well by the calculation of the carbon 14 within it.

Also charcoal from ancient cooking fires is one of the commonest substances which yields a carbon 14 date. The date derived from a piece of charcoal would indicate the time of death of the tree from which that piece of wood had been derived. It might have been many years later that some ancient hunter picked up the dried branch and threw it on his fire. It was also possible that the normal process of absorption of carbon 14 and its disintegration might have been interfered with in some samples, thereby causing error in dating calculations.

Water, percolating through soil in which such beds of charcoal are buried, might leach out some of the radioactive carbon and the hair root of a modern living plant might be incorporated in an ancient sample of charcoal.

One of the major hazards to setting dates by radioactive evidence grew out of the progress of atomic science itself. During the time when the United States was testing atom bombs at Frenchman's Flat in Nevada, great amounts of radioactive matter were thrown into the air. This was to become the fallout material which has caused so much controversy among both scientists and laymen. In some instances, radioactive particles travel several times around the earth before they finally settle. The winds in the Northern Hemisphere are generally westerly. The prevailing winds in the United States move from the northwest to the southeast. These winds drifted the radioactive particles across Chicago, Ann Arbor (Michigan), and New York City where laboratories had been set up to measure carbon 14. A scientist trying to count the pulsations of an ancient piece of carbon 14 found that radioactive particles of dust and other matter completely befuddled his delicate calculations. Most of the laboratories simply had to stop their program of carbon 14 sampling until the radioactive air from the bomb blasts had dissipated and passed. Carbon 14 scientists were aware of the problem of fallout long before health officials were concerned with its menace.

The radioactive calendar of carbon 14 was not perfect. There were laboratory difficulties and possible stumbling blocks in some of the samples themselves, but nevertheless carbon 14 provided the best system yet for answering the question, "How old?" Professor Kirk Bryan, for example, had judged that the Sandia Cave had first been occupied by early American hunters about 25,000 years ago. He made this deduction on the basis of movements of the last glacial period. A carbon 14 date derived from a piece of mammoth tusk from the Sandia level of the cave gave a date of 26,000 years before the present. Professor Bryan had been remarkably accurate in his geological guess.

Charcoal from the campfires of Folsom men near Lubbock, Texas, dated back 9,883 years. This was also very close to the date which had previously been determined for the Folsom hunters. However, a carbon 14 date from a "Clovis," which is an early type of Folsom camp site near Lewisville, Texas, yielded a date in excess of 37,000 years B.P. Carbon 14 dates are reckoned as "B.P."—before the present. The Lewisville, Texas, date seems much too early. When a number of carbon 14 dates for the same kind of life such as those identifiable as Folsom man all fall within certain limits, the archaeologist is satisfied that he has pinpointed on his calendar the time at which that kind of American actually lived. When there is one sour note such as the Lewisville date, he suspects that something has gone wrong with the sample.

As the first scattering of carbon 14 datings began to come in, not only from the United States but also from South America, Europe, Asia, and Africa, the order of human events began to form a recognizable pattern. Especially in the Americas, there were at first many wide gaps in the story. The easily recognizable Ice Age hunters such as Folsom and Sandia had lived here more than 10,000 years before the present time. Carbon 14 datings from pieces of peat and soggy wood incorporated in the glacial deposits themselves dated the movements of the glacial tongues of ice and the other cosmic happenings which took place at the same time as the glaciations. Archaeologists and geologists were able to reconstruct very exactly not only the doings of man but also an exact timetable of the climatic changes and glacial happenings upon which these early human beings were so dependent. The last glacial period, or Wisconsin glaciation, came to an end about 8,000 years ago. The Ice Age animals so typical of this epoch also became extinct at about that time.

Further carbon 14 dates will probably indicate that not all of the Ice Age beasts became extinct at the same time. The bison which the Folsom hunters habitually killed are varieties now extinct. Apparently the modern type of bison which we mistakenly call "buffalo" appeared soon after the end of the Wisconsin glaciation. An earlier hunter, Clovis man, habitually killed mammoths. The mammoth probably died out in both the New and the Old Worlds about nine or ten thousand years ago, some time before the Ice Age bison became extinct.

The picture of the earliest varieties of Ice Age Americans became more clearly etched on the carbon 14 calendar than some events of later times. Archaeologists already knew that the great centers of the Mexicans, the Mayas and the Andeans, had flourished some time after the birth of Christ. By stratigraphy and dead reckoning, archaeologists had pushed back the beginnings of agriculture a few centuries before the birth of Christ. There the information seemed to end, leaving a tremendous gap between the early Ice Age hunters and those later people who had begun to grow agricultural products and to make pottery. This gap in our knowledge of early America led some scientists to suggest that the Ice Age hunters had died off at the end of the glacial period as had the animals which they hunted. These theorists reasoned that the human story had then begun all over again, with later migrations of more civilized people. The later migrants formed the so-called "archaic" cultures from which evolved such great civilizations as the Mound Builders, the Pueblo peoples of the American Southwest, and the Mayas and Andeans of Central and South America.

The scientists who postulated this chain of events should have had more confidence in the ability of mankind to survive changes which would have driven a lesser species to extinction. Carbon 14 dates from a place called Bat Cave, near the town of Magdalena in New Mexico, showed that a primitive kind of corn was being cultivated there some 5,000 years ago. Other carbon 14 dates derived from deeply buried campfires in such places as Texas, Wyoming, and Nebraska showed that people were living in these areas in the millennia between the time of the Folsom hunters and the era of agriculture. Nor was the area east of the Mississippi devoid of human beings during the gap. Carbon 14 dates from an ancient fish weir beneath Boston, Massachusetts, showed that human beings had caught fish there 5,717 years ago. A cave shelter south of St. Louis in southern Illinois yielded carbon 14 dates equivalent to 9,882 B.P.

Gradually archaeologists were able to discover how men lived in America from the time following the end of the glacial period up till modern times. Some of these early Americans were hunters. They hunted those animals which survived the great extinction at the end of the Ice Age. They made recognizable lance points and lived much as their forebears had done.

But many people who inhabited America during the

"in-between era" after the Glacial Age were not hunters or, at best, they hunted only small game. Probably, after the Ice Age, there was not enough game in many parts of the country to support a way of life which depended solely on hunting. Instead of hunting, many of these early Americans gathered different types of vegetable food. The human mammal is very adaptable and also omnivorous. It was this fact which probably accounted for the survival of human beings after the great changes which took place at the end of the Ice Age. If human beings have to, they can eat almost anything. Apparently these groups of early American food gatherers did just that. They ate roots and tubers and picked berries. They snared small game and birds and pounded up grasshoppers and gophers with whatever else they could find that looked edible into a delectable pulp.

Usually, evidence of the existence of these peoples is found in and around fire pits where they roasted their food. Flat stones upon which they mashed or ground their food, and stones with flattened facets which were held in the hand and used to do the pounding, are found scattered around the charcoal of the campfires. Occasionally there are found crude choppers with which they dismembered small animals or split wood. Usually there is no more archaeological evidence than this. Most of these food-gathering groups had no projectile points, or at least stone-tipped ones. Their life was simple. From the carbon 14 dates of many of their campfires, it is obvious that their kind of life went on in America for a very long time.

Another laboratory dating method, which may be useful in supplying data which the carbon 14 method cannot, was developed by Dr. George Kennedy of the Institute of Geophysics at the University of California at Los Angeles. Dr. Kennedy calls his method "thermoluminescence."

This system, Dr. Kennedy claims, can date burned rock ranging from that which is fifteen years old to that which is two million years old—a range much wider than the one carbon 14 can serve.

Dr. Kennedy's system is based upon the examination of the change in the surface of stone which is caused by extreme heat. The thermal glow emitted by an object when heated to temperatures of from 100° to 400° centigrade is proportionate to the number of years which have elapsed since that same object was heated to that same temperature in an ancient campfire. By examining a blackened fragment of rock from some ancient fire hearth, Dr. Kennedy can tell the exact year at which the fire heated the rock and altered its surface. He does so by reheating the sample under laboratory conditions and observing the curve of thermoluminescence and the radioactivity of the sample and plotting them on a graph. He has checked his burned-rock calendar on many samples of lava of known date which were heated by the cosmic fires in the interior of the earth.

Dr. Kennedy's calendar has already filled in some of the gaps in the time scale which the carbon 14 method left. In places where the radioactive carbon samples may be polluted or faulty, Dr. Kennedy's calendar will give exact dates. Contamination of the air with radioactive fallout from man-made blasts has no effect whatsoever on this kind of calendar.

By these ingenious devices, archaeology has come of age as an exact science. Archaeologists dealing only with scattered bones, fragments of charcoal, and burned rock can now discover a historical continuity with as much assurance as the historian who works with written records. If anything, radioactive archaeology is more accurate than written history which is often set down by a biased person or one so close to the facts that his reports lack perspective. Laboratory reports are not biased. Archaeological history produced from tree rings, carbon 14, and burned stone is as exact as laboratory techniques can make it.

4

How Did the Americans Come?

THE QUESTION, "How old?" has been largely answered by the meticulous calculations of astronomers, chemists, and physicists. There are, however, other pressing questions to be answered before the complete story of early America is known. If the first Americans did not originate in the New World, they migrated to these shores from the Old World continents. The first arrivals came to America about 30,000 years ago during the closing phases of the last or Wisconsin glaciation. But how did these migrants get here?

"How did they come?" was a question more difficult to answer than "When did they arrive?" The bones of animals they killed, the charcoal from burned-out campfires or the blackened surfaces of rocks could reveal the time at which these things happened. However, the "how" of their happening seemed locked forever in the minds of ancient Americans who left no written records. Even their bodies have not been recovered.

Of course, a number of the early investigators answered the question with childlike conviction. Some of the first to study the Mayan ruins stated simply that the Mayas were an offshoot of the ancient Egyptians. Lord Kingsborough, an early worker on the antiquities of the Mexicans, spent his life demonstrating that the Mexicans were the descendants of the Ten Lost Tribes of Israel and published a long series of Mexican manuscripts to prove his point. None of these enthusiasts, however, demonstrated how the Egyptians or the descendants of Israel could have sailed their frail ships across the wide reaches of the middle Atlantic to land on these shores and found a great American civilization.

Furthermore, as the fascinating tale of American beginnings became clear, there were two insurmountable difficulties to such an easy theory of American origins. The first of these was that the earliest Americans came to the New World many thousands of years before the dynastic Egyptian civilization was extant in the Valley of the Nile. The first Americans were simple hunters living a kind of life which has been called "Upper Paleolithic" in Europe. Another difficulty was that archaeologists had begun to find a succession of American cultures which had led in gradually developing stages to the climax of the high civilizations of the Mexican, Mayan, and Andean areas. The great civilized centers of early America were not transplantations from the Old World. They were American developments. But it was still not known how the earliest forebears of these civilizations came to America.

A number of theories were evolved and tested to try to trace this greatest of ancient migrations.

Linguistic evidence is often used to follow the movements of people. Long after the human memory of tribal movements has been lost, anthropologists can trace migrations through similarities in language. Unfortunately, in America linguists were unable to find similarities between American languages and those of Europe or Asia—with one exception, the language of the Eskimos. Alaskan Eskimos and Siberian Eskimos speak an almost identical tongue. However, as the Eskimos even today pass back and forth across the polar regions, the similarity could be of very recent origin.

A number of early investigators professed to see similarity or identity between the languages of the Aztecs and the Chinese. With real linguistic study, however, these similarities disappeared. No linguistic trail of evidence has ever been discovered which would reveal the origins of the first Americans.

Physical evidence also is general and inconclusive. American Indians today, presumably descendants of Ice Age Americans, are decidedly Mongoloid in appearance. Many American Indians possess the "Mongoloid fold" on the inner canthus of the eye which is the hallmark of the Mongoloid stock. A large percentage of Indians also have the "Mongoloid spot," which is a splash of bluish-black pigment located on the lower part of the back just over the sacrum. This curious Mongoloid spot is much commoner among Indian babies and tends to disappear with adulthood. It is also a peculiarity of the Mongoloid peoples. Generally also, the American Indian has black straight hair, dark brown eyes, and the reddish or brownish-red skin pigment of the typical Mongoloid. When an American visitor to an Indian encampment sees a baby held in his mother's arms, the visitor often remarks, "He looks just like a little Chinese baby." This is no accident. Although the American Indians vary widely in appearance, there is no doubt that in general characteristics they are Mongoloid.

Unfortunately, Mongoloid or near-Mongoloid people are found all the way from the southernmost Pacific islands to the Siberian Arctic. Mongoloid mixtures also occur in northern Europe. Groups of Mongoloid people moved into northern Europe and the polar regions in early times. The invasions by such people as the Huns brought Mongoloid stock into the heart of Europe.

Considering all these Mongoloid movements and mixtures, it is difficult, if not impossible, to try to pinpoint the origin of the American Indians by means of their physical type alone. However, the fact that the earliest Americans were generally Mongoloid tends to cause us to focus our attention upon the Pacific area where the Mongoloids are concentrated.

However, even in the Pacific there is abundant evidence that Caucasian types existed at a very early date. Early Caucasians are represented by such present-day remnants as the Ainus, who still live in the northern Japanese island of Hokkaido. The Ainus, usually called the "hairy Ainu" to distinguish them from the surrounding Mongoloids who have little or no body hair, are extremely different from the other Asiatic people. Physically, the Ainu are much closer to the European races. The Ainu apparently represent a very early movement of these Caucasian and non-Mongoloid peoples into eastern Asia.

Certain anthropologists profess to see, in the American Indians, evidences of a very early migration of Ainu-like stock. Such an early migration would perhaps be a part of the same eastward movement from some Asiatic center which brought the Ainu into the Japanese islands. There is no doubt that the migration of these people in eastern Asia took place very early. Whether Caucasoid Ainu got to America is another question.

Physical anthropologists may argue that modern American Indians are descendants of original Ainu-like migrants overawed by later Mongoloid travelers. However, even these speculations do not answer the question, "How did they come?"

Even though linguistic and physical arguments seem to point to a Pacific ocean route, a number of scientists have tried to demonstrate that the first Americans came by way of the Atlantic. Chiefly this was because, in more recent times, early Europeans with very primitive sailing craft did come that way. Columbus, of course, made a landfall on these shores in 1492. At least 600 years earlier than Columbus, the Norsemen had found their way across the North Atlantic from Iceland to Greenland and thence to Labrador. The Norse landing in Greenland is recorded as happening in the year 985 A.D. However, there are evidences that even earlier Viking voyagers had penetrated into Hudson Bay or possibly down to the New England coast. The Kensington Stone, a slab inscribed with runic writing found in 1898 near Kensington in Minnesota, has been claimed as evidence that Scandinavian peoples had penetrated that far into the North American continent as early as the fourteenth century. The runic inscription tells a tale of bloodshed and privation. Translated with some reconstruction it reads:

"[We are] 8 Goths [Swedes] and 22 Norwegians on [an] exploration journey from Vineland round about the West. We had camp by [a lake with] 2 skerries one day's journey north from this stone. We were [out] and fished one day. After we came home [we] found 10 [of our] men red with blood [scalped] and dead. AV[E] M[ARIA] save [us] from evil. [We] 10 of [our party] by the sea to look after our ships [or ship] 14 days' journey from the island [in the] year [of our Lord] 1362."

Some scholars claim that the Kensington evidence is a cleverly contrived fake.

Near Newport, Rhode Island, is a circular stone tower purportedly constructed by Viking colonists. It was here that the poet Longfellow viewed the burial which he immortalized in "A Skeleton in Armor." Some archaeologists have claimed to have found Norse axes and other evidences of Scandinavian landings on Cape Cod and even farther south. Even if these evidences are authentic—and there is considerable doubt about most of them—and however early such Scandinavian penetrations took place, they cannot account for the first migration of people to America. When the first Viking explorer reached the foggy shores of Labrador, there is no doubt that he found people—American Indians.

Some have argued that if the Vikings came that way, why could not some earlier northern European have made their migration across the North Atlantic by way of Iceland, Greenland, and thence to Labrador? But if we consider the time at which the earliest migration must have taken place, the North Atlantic route theory becomes ridiculous. None of the early peoples of the Old World had developed any kind of boat thirty thousand years ago. They probably crossed rivers and narrow lakes by sitting astride a log and paddling with a branch. With such crude methods of water transportation a voyage from Europe to Iceland to Greenland would have been impossible.

An English zoologist, H. E. Forrest, in his book *The Atlantean Continent,* postulated a land bridge crossing the North Atlantic from Scandinavia through Iceland to

North America. It was across this bridge, Forrest argued, that plants and fresh-water fish, making their way from stream to stream, moved from Europe to America. Why not human beings also? Forrest drew upon the legend of a lost Atlantean continent to prove his point. Unfortunately for such an intriguing solution, there was no geological evidence that any such Atlantic land bridge existed as late as the Pleistocene, which is the time of Man. Forrest's land bridge, consisting of the lost continent of Atlantis, is only one of several mythical continents which supposedly sank beneath the waters of the seven seas. So fascinating is the question of possible lost continents that even today a number of people believe that the first Americans originated on or came by way of one of them. New books are written on the subject almost every year.

The most popular of these theories deals with the lost continent of Atlantis. This continent, presumably located in the South Atlantic, was first mentioned by Plato, in two Socratic treatises, the *Timaeus* and the *Critias,* which he wrote about 355 B.C. In these dialogues, Plato was trying to make a number of points about principles of government. According to his account, the continent of Atlantis was located beyond the Pillars of Hercules, the Greek name for the Strait of Gibraltar. On it was a circular city fifteen miles in diameter called Basilea. It was joined to the sea by an inner and outer harbor and there was an irrigated plain beyond it. Plato describes the appearance of the city (with its minerals and elephants) and recounts the story of the ten kings, sons of the god Poseidon, who ruled Atlantis. He never described ships, buildings, or any other facet of Atlantis in cultural terms unfamiliar to him. He was using this mythical land with its mythical ten kings to make a number of social points. The Atlanteans, at first virtuous, fell into a moral decline and became evil and greedy. Consequently Zeus, the ruler of all the gods, called the gods to a meeting in his palace. The dialogue ends with the words: ". . . and Zeus spake thus . . ." We never know what Zeus spoke, inasmuch as Plato had made his point. As far as he was concerned, Atlantis was finished.

Unfortunately, Atlantis was not finished. The tale was picked up by writers in the fifteenth century when rumors of new lands ran riot. In the seventeenth century Sir Francis Bacon wrote *The New Atlantis* and located the land in America. But the legend of the lost continent was really launched in modern times through a book written by a Philadelphia lawyer named Ignatius Donnelly and published by Harpers in 1882. Donnelly called his book *Atlantis: The Antediluvian World;* by 1890 there were twenty-three American and twenty-six English editions. If a story appears in print, and especially in a book, many people believe that it must be true, and other enthusiasts took up the story of Atlantis and carried it on. In the early 1900s, book after book dealing with the Lost Continent of Atlantis appeared.

Donnelly argued that since the people and cultures of America, Europe, and the Near East were similar, they must all have originated in Atlantis. The American Indians and the early Europeans both came from Atlantis, Donnelly said, because they both had flood legends, used spears, and practiced marriage and divorce. Anthropologists have shown that these are cultural attributes of almost all people. The same argument could be used to prove connections between Africa, Australia, and Europe.

Equally spurious is Donnelly's "proof" of the derivation of Mayan writing from Egyptian hieroglyphics. Donnelly evolved a table paralleling Egyptian signs with the phonetic Mayan characters as given by Bishop Landa, the Spanish bishop of Mérida in Yucatán. Donnelly apparently did not know that the Mayan alphabet which the Indians gave to Bishop Landa was a purposeful hoax concocted by them as an act of revenge against the bishop for burning their native books. Even the fake Mayan alphabet presented such glaring differences from the Egyptian that Donnelly had to concoct "intermediate forms."

Not content with this, author Donnelly made a comparative table to show that Chinese and Otomi, a Mexican language, are related and therefore both derivative of the language of the Lost Atlanteans. Both Chinese and Otomi are languages in which the pitch at which a word or syllable is pronounced determines the meaning. So also are many of the languages of Africa. Not only that, but Donnelly picked Chinese words to suit his purpose and some of his Chinese parallels do not appear in the Chinese dictionary at all. Even a casual study of Chinese and Otomi shows that the two languages are not related. Nevertheless, many Atlantean authors of modern times state as a proven fact that Otomi is archaic Chinese or Japanese.

As each writer sought to improve upon the account of his predecessor, Atlantis was peopled with strange beings who, long before our time, had marvelous metals, airships, submarines, and knew and used atomic power. Almost incidentally these authors, such as George Wolfe to mention one among many, recount that when the great continent of Atlantis sank beneath the waters of the oceans, certain survivors from the submerged land came to American shores and became the first inhabitants of this virgin wilderness.

The idea that Atlantis has sunk beneath the water seems to add spice to the tale. Also, it is argued, if the continent is gone, how can it be proved that it never existed? Thus the fascination of sunken treasure and submarine cities is added to the interest in antiquity.

Needless to say, there is no geological or anthropological evidence to indicate that any large island or continent ever existed beyond the "Pillars of Hercules" within the time span of the existence of human life on our own continent.

Not in the least daunted, the German archaeologist and diver, Jurgen Spanuth, in 1953, claimed to have found the submerged continent beneath the waters of the North Sea beyond the island of Heligoland. Spanuth even announced the discovery of a curved wall on the ocean floor, a remnant of the circular city wall of Basilea, the capital of Atlantis itself. Other divers disappointingly could find no traces of the sunken city.

It seems useless for the anthropologist to point out that the North Sea was, for most of the Ice Age, a marshy valley. It was only at the very end of the Ice Age that the waters invaded this valley, which is the floor of the English Channel we know today. The last human beings to walk the fens of the valley were simple fishers and hunters still living a Mesolithic type of life. There is plentiful evidence of these fisher folk. There is no sign of any great cities. Even Plato, in his imaginative tale, did not place the Lost Atlantis in the North Sea or in the North Atlantic where H. E. Forrest wanted it.

But people like stories of sunken cities and lost continents. Atlantean societies still flourish in the United States, publish books, and hold annual meetings. One of the most active of the groups dedicated to the idea of Atlantis is the Société d'Études Atlantéenes in Paris. They have printed Atlantean stamps and hold Atlantean meetings. At a meeting of the Société in 1927 a rival threw stink bombs into the meeting to break up the conclave. Thus acrimonious politics has entered the field of lost continents.

Almost equal in popularity to Atlantis is another supposedly perished continent called Mu. The legend of Mu (under a different name) first appeared in a book written by an imaginative mythologist named Lewis Spence, who in 1911 also wrote of a continent which he called Antillia in the Caribbean. But it was an uninhibited writer named James Churchward who made the most of the alleged continent in the Pacific. Churchward's book, *The Lost Continent of Mu,* published in its "final" form in 1929, is a classic of misconception and surmise. His sources for most of the information about Mu were the "Naacal Tablets" which had been given to him by a mysterious Hindu priest. This priest, whom nobody else ever saw, or heard of, also translated the Naacal Tablets and gave Churchward other information about the life and days of the Muians.

Mu was supposed to have existed in the Pacific Ocean. It was purportedly of roughly triangular shape with one corner resting upon the Hawaiian Islands and a southern tip extending into the South Pacific as far as Easter Island. Mu was supported by "gas belts," a very unusual base for a chunk of solid land. When the gas belts collapsed, the continent of Mu sank bubbling beneath the waters of the Pacific.

Before Mu sank, it was supposed to have spewed forth a vast quantity of animals, things, and people. Each account of the lost continent of Mu became more fantastic as each author improved upon the original ideas of Lewis Spence and James Churchward. Curiously enough, the constant shift of ideas seemed only to increase the credulity of those who avidly read about things Muian. Dinosaurs and early peoples were included in a fantastic mélange of culture. Geologists who entered the controversy pointed out in vain that dinosaurs had become extinct long before any human beings ever existed on the face of the earth. But the Muians persisted in writing more and more nonsense about the now disappeared continent. Churchward professed to be able to read the Muian alphabet. He said that the letter "m" in Muian is a rectangle, and that a rectangle appearing anywhere in nature stands for Mu, and is incontrovertible proof that the Muians had been there. According to this argument, the face of a brick, which is rectangular in outline, is the letter "m" of the Muian alphabet and demonstrates that the Muians originated bricks.

This curious logic was used by the adherents of the Muian theory to prove that the American Indians were the descendants of those survivors of the Lost Continent of Mu who had escaped from the sinking island before it was completely submerged. And then for good measure they also derived the Chinese and even the ancient Egyptians from Mu. Inasmuch as Mu has now sunk and disappeared, they argue, you cannot disprove the theory.

There is no more geological evidence for the existence of the continent of Mu in the Pacific than there is for Atlantis in the Atlantic. Nor do we need to derive the first Americans from any such fantastic continent as the dinosaur-inhabited Mu. However, anthropological arguments and geological denials have not dampened the enthusiasm of the followers of Mu or that of the followers of Atlantis. On the contrary, publications and meetings to discuss the possibilities of Mu seem to be on the increase. Most of these activities are centered around Los Angeles, California, but are by no means limited to that area.

The theories about Atlantis and Mu were both given an unexpected lift early in the twentieth century by Paul Schliemann, grandson of the famous Heinrich Schliemann who discovered and excavated Homeric Troy. In 1912, Paul Schliemann, apparently thinking to carry on the family tradition at any cost, gave the newspapers a sensational story of his finding some fabulous archaeological treasures inscribed in Phoenician script. The script told of the continent of Atlantis beyond the Pillars of Hercules. Paul Schliemann also announced the discovery of a Chaldean (that is, from Mesopotamia) document "which came from Tibet." This told of the collapse and sinking of Mu. When asked how he had come upon these wonderful things, Schliemann averred that they had been sealed in an owl-headed jar and left to him by his grandfather with instructions that the jar be opened after the latter's death. But the owl-headed vase never found its way into a museum. Young Schliemann was unable to produce either the vase or the Chaldean document to substantiate his story.

The Mu and Atlantis adherents have recently joined forces. They have announced that the Muians dug a canal through the Andes Mountains of South America into the basin of the Amazon. Through this canal, Muian ships established trade with the continent of Atlantis! If one contemplates the outlines of the Andean cordillera, it becomes clear that the building of such a canal is an engineering feat of which only Muians would be capable.

Atlantis and Mu are not the only lost continents to be suggested as the place of origin of the first Americans. A third candidate is the lost continent of Lemuria. Curiously enough, the lost Lemuria was actually suggested by two scientists. About 1875 these scientists, Haeckel and Blanford, became interested in the distribution of lemurs in Asia and Africa. The lemur is one of those primates that have a few characteristics in common with man. Fossils of extinct forms of lemurs have been found in many parts of the Old World. Living lemurs occur only in southern Asia, Madagascar, and the adjacent coast of East Africa. Because of this distribution, the two zoologists advanced the notion that a land bridge or subcontinent might have existed connecting India, the East Indies, and the east coast of Africa. They called this body of land Lemuria.

It was very soon discovered that lemurs had once existed in southeast Asia, North Africa, and even Europe. There was no necessity for postulating a lost continent of Lemuria. But the damage had already been done. Here was a lost continent that had actually been suggested by scientists.

The chief champion of Lemuria was Heliona P. Blevatsky, who wrote a book on the subject. Madame Blevatsky peopled the lost Lemuria with what she called "root races." These root races were fantastic by any biological standards. The Lemurians proper were beetle-browed, hermaphroditic giants who laid eggs. Madame Blevatsky professed a contempt for the "monkey theories" of human evolution. Instead, in the original continent of Lemuria, the root races had no sex whatsoever. Then, when the situation became blemished by the introduction of sex, evolution worked in reverse. The Lemurians, some of whom had four arms and an extra eye in the back of their heads, interbred with lower beasts and the human form regressed to those of the hairy animals.

Madame Blevatsky catalogued the Atlanteans as the "Fourth Root Race" which grew from the Third Root Race. It was from the Fourth Root Race that the Mongoloids and incidentally the American Indians were derived. All the root races were possessed of what she called "Cosmic Consciousness."

The United States and especially California has been involved in the Lemuria controversy because of a variant theory which places Lemuria in the Pacific Ocean in the spot usually reserved for Mu. Just how Lemuria became substituted for Mu is not clear. However, this version usually appears in connection with the "Mount Shasta Legend." According to the story, popularized in 1894 by a novel, *A Dweller on Two Planets,* by F. S. Oliver, survivors from Lemuria made their way to the coast and gathered on Mount Shasta in northern California. Even today, members of Los Angeles occult groups will assure you that Lemurians in white robes can be seen on Mount Shasta holding secret conclaves in the full of the moon. Disappointingly enough, an ordinary anthropologist or layman who does not possess mystic powers cannot see these things even if he searches all over Mount Shasta.

Another lost continent which has given anthropologists considerable trouble has been named Gondwanaland. This was supposed to have existed in the area which is now the East Indies of the South Pacific and to stretch to Africa and South America. Recently also there has been much speculation and writing about the continent of Antarctica. Antarctica is frozen at the present time but this was not always so. How can it be proven, argue the advocates of lost continent theories, that Antarctica was not the original home of the American Indian?

But if one is not irrevocably dedicated to deriving the first Americans from sunken continents which never existed, there are other possibilities more anthropologically acceptable. One of the most interesting of these is called the "Chinese junk theory." This postulates that the American Indians are descendants of the crew of a Chinese junk which drifted across the Pacific in early times and cast up living survivors on American shores.

The idea received lively support a number of years ago because of two indicative facts. The first was that the American Indians are generally Mongoloid. The second was that the Japanese current, which swings in a great arc northward and eastward across the northern Pacific, would carry any flotsam such as a wrecked ship across the ocean in an easterly direction. The many glass fish-net floats which break loose from fishermen in the Japanese islands show the direction and movement of the Japanese current. These glass floats are picked up along the Aleutian shores and on the beaches of the northwest coast of North America. It seems logical to suppose that a wrecked boat could be carried in the same way by the Japanese current.

Anthropologists were especially impressed by the fact that when Captain Cook, the early explorer, in 1778 voyaged along this same northwest coast, he found the American Indians there in possession of items which seemed oriental. Later in the twentieth century, when anthropologists studied such tribes as the Haida and Kwakiutl among the Northwest Coast Indians, they found the natives using Chinese coins and Chinese bronze dangles for ornaments. Anthropologists also pointed out that ornamented wooden dance masks of these same Northwest Coast Indians often featured a large mustache. As American Indians do not usually have hair on their faces, a handlebar mustache is a curious detail. The hairy Ainu of the northern Japanese island of Hokkaido, however, do grow luxurious mustaches. Also, the Ainu manufacture decorated blankets or capes and also hats which they wear as ceremonial attire. The Northwest Coast Indians also make shoulder blankets and hats. Even the designs of the Indian blankets are similar to those of eastern Asia. Ceremonies eulogizing the bear are suggestively similar among the Ainu and the Northwest Coast aborigines of North America. A junkload of shipwrecked Asiatics might explain the presence of all of these interesting cultural phenomena in North America.

Intriguing as the Chinese junk theory is, it does not account for the arrival of the first Americans. Chinese junks were not developed until the centuries after Christ. It must be remembered that the earliest human arrivals in the New World came at a time when boats were unknown even in Asia. Even if there was some kind of craft 30,000 years ago, it is extremely dubious that any men could survive during the voyage of very many weeks necessary to drift along the Japanese current to our Northwest Coast. But even if some Asiatics managed to survive the trip in a Chinese junk, they would not have been the first arrivals on these shores, for they would have found American Indians already here.

In considering floating ships as a solution to the mystery of American origins, we discover a number of intriguing possibilities. One of the most plausible is called the Easter Island theory. Attention has been focused in the direction of Easter Island in the South Pacific by the classic cruise of the balsawood raft, "Kon-Tiki." Thor Heyerdahl, the skipper of "Kon-Tiki," has suggested many fascinating connections between Easter Island and other South Pacific islands and the coast of South America.

Long before the voyage of the "Kon-Tiki," it had been thought that Easter Island might have been the stepping stone in the vast waters of the South Pacific by which early human beings first came to American shores. Easter Island, so named because of its discovery on Easter Day, 1787, does seem to be the most logical route by which seafaring natives could have made the trip to America.

A glance at a chart of South Pacific waters reveals such distances of water between Easter Island and the nearest other groups of South Pacific islands that it would seem impossible for any early human beings to have been able to make the voyage. This tiny dot of land lies 1,600 miles from Polynesian Mangareva and 2,200 miles from the South American coast. But Easter Island was populated by natives when the first Europeans discovered it. Even though the Easter Islanders had very primitive boats when they were first discovered, obviously some human beings had made the trip in pre-European times.

The journey had probably been made possible by the outrigger canoe, a seagoing device which originated in the South Pacific. Dugout canoes, hollowed from the trunk of a single tree, are generally unstable craft and certainly unfit for ocean travel. However, by rigging an additional log parallel to one side of the dugout by means of two poles tied at right angles across the thwarts of the canoe, a great degree of stability is achieved. An outrigger may be placed on one side of the dugout canoe or on both, in which case it is called a "double outrigger." The outrigger stabilizes the canoe by its buoyancy and by leverage.

With outriggers of this sort, South Pacific natives made regular voyages from island to island. The remarkable voyages, some of them over 2,000 miles of open ocean, achieved by these South Pacific mariners are a matter of historical record. They used celestial navigation and followed remarkable charts which they constructed by tying sticks together in series. They carried coconuts and fished for food. They caught rain water as they traveled.

There is no doubt that the outrigger canoe was the means by which most of the South Pacific islands were originally populated. The Hawaiian Islands were populated from the middle Pacific. The Easter Islanders are purely Polynesian in origin, as evidenced by their Polynesian speech and typical Polynesian culture whose gods, houses, stone platforms, cannibalism, and other features resemble those of the other islanders farther west. Easter Island was populated by means of outrigger canoes, probably from the Solomon Islands.

If South Pacific natives made these prodigious voyages in historic times and obviously also in earlier periods, why not this means for the entry of the first human beings into America? In the vast South Pacific, Easter Island is a pinpoint of land only 10 by 13 miles in size. If early outrigger mariners were skillful enough to find it, the voyage from Easter Island to the coast of South America should have been relatively simple.

The Easter Island theory was furthered by connections which archaeologists were able to make. Two graves were discovered in Peru which contained typical Andean material and South Sea island clubs. These wooden clubs or *patu,* as they are called in the Pacific islands, are made of a very hard wood and are pointed at the end so that they can be used as thrusting or clubbing weapons. The patu is typical of the South Pacific. It is not at all typical of the Andean coast. Because of the extreme aridity of the Peruvian coast, wooden objects and also textiles are often preserved. Archaeologists argue that sword clubs could only have been brought by Easter Islanders traveling in outrigger canoes.

Archaeologists also noticed a similarity between large basalt stone carvings in Easter Island and megalithic statues in the Andean area. Also, in the islands closest to Easter Island, there are terraced hills, apparently built for defense, which bear a remarkable similarity to terraced mountain ridges in the Peruvian area and to terraced pyramids in Central America. The construction of pyramids, which are built up in steps or terraces, is an outstanding characteristic of the great centers of American culture from the Andes northward through Mexico and into the Mississippi Valley of the United States. Those who advocated the Easter Island theory held that the practice of building terraced religious monuments must have been brought to American shores by some of the earliest migrants.

Other backers of the Easter Island theory of migration

pointed out parallels between the art of Middle America and that of southeastern Asia. Dr. Grafton Elliot Smith, an eminent physician, as early as 1924 published an essay entitled, "Elephants and Ethnologists." The title is suggestive of the motifs which Dr. Smith traced from southeast Asia to the New World. He compared motifs found in the Mayan area, Cambodia, Indochina, and throughout southeastern Asia. He pointed out that on certain Mayan temples such as those at the sites of Palenque and Copán, the original Mayan builders had sculptured elephant heads. He argued that the Mayas could not have known what an elephant looked like unless it had been described to them by islanders who had come across the Pacific. Dancing figures, headdresses, and other motifs appearing on Mayan temples seemed exactly to parallel sculptural details on Buddhist monuments of southeastern Asia. More cautious anthropologists pointed out that the elephants sculptured on Mayan temples might be representations of the American tapir, a relative of the rhinoceros. Dr. Smith replied that the Mayan animal heads had tusks which the American tapir does not. The Asiatic elephant, however, has tusks. He also said that the proboscis was closer in appearance to the trunk of an elephant than to the snout of a tapir.

Migrants from southeastern Asia could have brought with them art motifs including the elephant, megalithic stone carvings, terraced pyramids, and even the idea of building in stone. This would also explain the distribution of these developments in America. The Andean coast seems a curious place for one of the high civilizations of the New World to have begun. If the original germs of this civilization came from the other side of the Pacific, however, the Andean location would be satisfactorily explained.

However, in the 1930s, further anthropological research in the South Pacific established with certainty that all the islands of the South Pacific were first occupied by men at a relatively late date. Thor Heyerdahl's archaeological digging during his second trip to Easter Island revealed the late occupation of Easter Island itself. Research showed that two waves of people had swept over these islands and in some places, perhaps, more than two waves. Different physical types of South Pacific natives were represented in the successive groups which occupied the Solomons, the Gilbert Islands, and Easter Island, giving evidence of successive movements of people from southeast Asia. Even the first of these movements, however, did not reach the islands of the southeastern Pacific until the centuries following the birth of Christ. Easter Island itself probably was unoccupied before 1000 A.D. Even if further digging should reveal that some intrepid human beings found these tiny islands a few centuries earlier, we must conclude that any outrigger canoes which Easter Islanders might have been able to land on the coast of South America landed on shores which were already populated.

Thor Heyerdahl and his raft, the "Kon-Tiki," demonstrated that a balsawood craft could make the trip from the Andean coast westward to the South Pacific islands. Heyerdahl certainly did demonstrate that a rudimentary boat of this sort could survive the voyage. The ocean currents generally move in a westerly direction and the winds are favorable. However, the trip of the "Kon-Tiki" does not solve our original problem. A raft built in the South Pacific islands would have great difficulty moving eastward to American shores. The outrigger canoe is a much better craft for the purpose. The outrigger can sail with ease against ocean currents and even make headway against adverse winds.

The "Kon-Tiki" expedition has demonstrated a number of parallels between American civilizations and those of the easternmost Pacific islands. Certainly we must postulate that in ancient times some boats, perhaps of the "Kon-Tiki" type, made the westward trip. The crews of rafts or outrigger canoes carried with them ideas which became implanted in the islands. The terraced pyramid, for instance, is apparently an indigenous American development and not an Asiatic one. It is much easier to explain the terraced hilltops of Asia as derived from America than vice versa. And the sweet potato is apparently American in origin. Sweet potatoes were being grown by Pacific islanders and Hawaiians when the first European sea captains landed on those islands. Perhaps some early "Kon-Tiki"-like voyagers carried sweet potatoes and introduced them in those islands.

But the cultural connections between the Pacific islands and Middle America must be regarded as a westward movement. Further archaeological research in the Pacific islands will certainly be profitable. There is no indication, however, that the American Indian came to this continent across the Pacific.

The voyage of the "Kon-Tiki" has been cited by those who believe in the lost continent of Mu as a modern demonstration of many such voyages undertaken by the Muians themselves. They regard Easter Island, as well as the Hawaiian Islands, as mountain-top remnants left above the surface when the great continent of Mu submerged. Needless to say, these theorists have added no evidence to the Easter Island hypothesis which would help us to reach any more certain conclusion about it.

Also, even today, many people have not abandoned the idea that the American Indians came from the Ten Lost Tribes of Israel. Others, still, contend that the first Indians were Chinese or Egyptians. If one does not stop to wonder how these early people got across vast stretches of ocean, then possibly these theories have some merit. Recently there has been a resurgence of the idea that the original American Indians were survivors of crews from the ships of Alexander the Great. Alexander is known to have collected a great fleet in the Gulf of Persia. When Alexander sickened and died in the city of Babylon in 323 B.C., he was ready to start on another great expedition to Asia. Nothing more was heard about these boats, their crews, or the admiral in command of them. If the Greek fleet actually reached American shores, it would have been a prodigious voyage indeed; and if the American Indians were derived from Macedonian sailors, there have been some fantastic physical changes in the few centuries since the Greeks landed. Even if we could get past these arguments, we can demonstrate conclusively that American Indians were here long before Alexander's fleet gathered in the Persian Gulf in the fourth century B.C.

It is not necessary to account for the origin of the American Indians through lost fleets or lost continents or even by fantastic voyages across open seas. The answer is more obvious and much closer at hand.

The front door to ancient America was the Bering Strait. Here the Seward Peninsula juts westward within 56 miles of the East Cape on the Siberian side. In this narrow strait lie the Diomede Islands. Big Diomede belongs to Russia, and Little Diomede is on the American side. On a clear day it is possible to see the Siberian coast from American land.

During the arctic winter, the Bering Strait freezes solid. Eskimos used to travel freely over the frozen ice by dog sled from Asia into North America and back again. The Eskimos on the Siberian coast have exactly the same language and the same culture as the American Eskimos. Of recent years, movement back and forth has almost ceased but the reasons are political and have nothing to do with the physical difficulties of the terrain.

It is not even necessary to postulate that the earliest American walked to the New World across sea ice. We know that the first migrants to the New World came during the last or Wisconsin glaciation. During each of the glaciations, tremendous amounts of moisture on the surface of the earth were locked up in the land masses in the form of glacial ice. According to the law of the conservation of matter, there is just so much of each kind of matter on this planet. If these thousands of cubic miles of water were turned into ice, there were that many fewer cubic miles of sea water in the oceans of the world. The ocean level during the period of greatest glaciations was probably about 60 meters lower than at present. Scientists differ in their estimates of the exact dimensions of the continental glaciers, but a reduction of only 20 meters in the level of the North Pacific would turn the relatively shallow Bering Strait into dry land.

At the time of the coming of first Americans, then, there was a Bering Isthmus, a neck of solid soil upon which they could walk over dry land into the New World. The bridge of land, the Bering Isthmus, which connected Asia with North America was not submerged until the end of the Wisconsin Period when the melting of the glacial ice had again raised the levels of the oceans. By that time, however, several waves of human migrants had already entered America's front door.

These first Americans were hunters. They hunted Ice Age animals typical of Wisconsin times. In New Mexico and in the American Southwest where evidences of these first Americans have been discovered, they were still living a hunting and wandering existence. The Sandia man and others of similar sort hunted mammoth, bison, horse, and camel—all animals typical of late Wisconsin times.

It seemed impossible to some that any such hunting American could have passed across the Bering Isthmus during glacial times. They argued that any human being would have perished in the arctic wastes of this northern land long before he could have made his way across hundreds of miles of glacial ice. Since the area around the North Pole is colder than the rest of America, it would seem that if there were glacial masses of ice in what is now Wisconsin and Colorado, it must have been frigid indeed in northern Alaska.

But this was not the case. Glacial geologists discovered that the Yukon Valley was ice free during much of the glacial time. In North America there were two major glacial masses. The largest of the continental glaciations lay over what is now Hudson Bay and extended its icy tongues southward at different times across the Great Lakes and into the northern portion of the United States. The other great glacial mass capped the Rocky Mountain uplift in a long narrow ice field extending north and south. Between these two masses of continental ice was a corridor which opened and closed as the glaciation diminished or increased.

It was thus possible for men to have made their way across the Bering Isthmus, through Alaska, and down into the heart of North America.

In 1941, the University of New Mexico sent a group of archaeologists, under the direction of the writer, northward into Alaska to test this theory. These archaeologists did not go without reason. Folsom points which had been found in New Mexico and other types of lance points which had been found elsewhere in the American West had also been discovered in the plains of Alberta and Saskatchewan in Canada. Other typical lance points of Ice Age hunters were found in Alaska not far from the Bering Strait.

In the Yukon Valley where gold miners have dredged great pits into the eternally frozen soil, archaeologists found the clues which they sought. In recent years, gold-mining companies have excavated great areas, for the most part with the use of hydraulic power. The miners wear their way down, with powerful streams of water, through a thick blanket of gray sand called "muck." The gold-bearing gravels lie beneath the muck. As the muck is frozen and is over 90 feet thick in some places, excavation presents a tremendous problem which the gold companies have solved with their hydraulic giants. They have laid bare whole acres of frozen ground, whereas the miners in the days of the Yukon rush were able to melt only tiny holes in the muck.

The hydraulic giants washed out more than gold nuggets. They also uncovered the bones of Ice Age animals —mammoths, bison, horses, and camels. The streaming courses of water also revealed the skeletons of tigers and wolves that had preyed upon the other animals.

Although the muck has been frozen since the Ice Age, there were remarkable instances of preservation. Most of the bodies of the animals had been torn and twisted by some violent cataclysm before being frozen in the enveloping muck. Yet in many cases fragments of ligaments, skin, hair, and even flesh adhered to the bones. Occasionally the whole shoulder or hind quarters of a mammoth were found preserved. The whole front portion of a baby mammoth complete with trunk and ears was found by the miners and shipped, under refrigeration, to the American Museum of Natural History.

The archaeologists also found mammoth meat which was still in an edible state. But they were less interested in the remarkable preservation than in the animals themselves. These late glacial age animals were the food supply of the first Americans. The bones frozen in the Alaskan muck were part of the background of the early American story. Perhaps, if the first migrants had passed this way, their bodies, too, might be frozen in the Yukon muck.

The frozen carcass of a Sandia man was not found, but the flint lance points of some of these earliest American hunters were discovered in one instance close beside the skull of an Alaskan tiger. These flint points were incontrovertible proof that human beings had been in the Yukon Valley during the Ice Age. Other points washed out of the muck indicated that still other hunters had walked the Yukon Valley at the end of the Ice Age. These people had seen the teeming animal herds and had lived upon their flesh. Carbon 14 dates of animal horns and tusks embedded in the muck are greater than 20,000 years.

Frozen mammoths of the same species are also found on the Siberian side of the Bering Strait. Elephants and other Ice Age animals moved freely back and forth across the land bridge between Alaska and Siberia. Indeed, it was across the Bering Isthmus that several species of animals moved in early glacial times to populate either the Old World or the New.

Early hunters in late glacial times could have moved from Siberia and into North America. From the evidence found in the Alaskan muck, it is certain that they did just that. Siberian scientists and American archaeologists still hope to find the frozen carcass of an early hunter. But it really matters very little whether the Russian archaeologists find a frozen man in the Siberian muck, or if the

Americans find a preserved body in the Yukon Valley. We could call either one of these the first American.

Almost certainly, the earliest human beings to enter the New World came across in straggling groups without ever realizing they were passing from one world to another. Some of them undoubtedly returned to Asia. Certainly, also, the first migrants to America came in several waves and over a long period of time. This would account for the evidences of different kinds of hunters which the archaeologists have identified in various parts of North America.

Still hunting the late glacial animals which were their food supply, these wandering groups moved down through Canada and into the western plains of North America. Along the foothills of the Rockies at the very edge of the glacial masses where the grass grew lushly, they found ideal hunting grounds. Some of them specialized in killing elephants. Others hunted only Ice Age bison; and then, as the hunting grew more difficult, they wandered south into Old Mexico and thence across the Isthmus of Panama and into South America. There were Ice Age animals also in South America. Evidence of very early Americans is also scantier there. However, at the very tip of South America, in southern Chile, Dr. Junius Bird, excavating in a cave, found evidence of hunters living there at the very end of the glacial period. This cave, called Palli Aikic Cave, in 1951 yielded a carbon 14 date of 8639 with a possible error of 451 years. At least that early, then, some groups of hunters had traveled the whole length of the Americas to populate its southernmost tip.

There is no longer any real mystery about how the first Americans came to the New World. We know how they came, and approximately when they came. Some of the other questions about American origins are not so easily answered.

5

The First Settlers

ARCHAEOLOGISTS are ordinarily interested in two things, people and culture. The culture of a given society is the sum total of everything its people make and say and do and think. Flint spear points provided the first information about the first Americans. By means of cultural material, the tools of the earliest Americans, the trail of the first comers was traced back to Alaska and thence to the Bering Strait. It was by means of charcoal from their cooking fires and bones of the animals which they killed that we were able to discover when they came across the Bering Isthmus. The cultural part of the story is now fairly clear.

But, as we have seen, at the great Folsom camp site of Lindenmeier in eastern Colorado and at the Clovis site near Clovis, New Mexico, no human skeletons were found. Nor were they found in the Sandia Cave. As archaeologists examined first one camping place and then another, the absence of human skeletal material became a nagging mystery. In the hundreds of areas in which the earliest Americans are known to have camped and lived, not a single fragment of human bone came to light.

This is all the more mysterious because primitive people are usually very careless with their dead. The earliest Americans were hunters and food gatherers. Hunters and food gatherers in other parts of the world normally buried their dead near their living places. Or, in some cases, they casually threw the deceased out with the garbage. And yet, on the American sites, no skeleton could be found, although archaeologists searched diligently.

It was not a question of preservation, for at Lindenmeier and at Clovis and in the Sandia Cave tons of animal bones were collected. In many cases the animal bones were highly fossilized. In the Alaskan muck, the carcasses of mammoths and bison and the other animals of the Ice Age were marvelously preserved. Why not the body of a man also?

Many archaeologists, working in Mexico and North and South America, had found and classified tens of thousands of implements made by the first Americans, but they never found so much as a bone from the hand which had made these implements. The first American himself was a nebulous figure. There were many stories and theories to account for his absence.

Some offered the suggestion that the earliest Americans cremated their dead. Some people and cultures dispose of the departed in this way. Cremation is practiced to this day.

Archaeologists know a lot about death. They spend a good deal of their time poking around tombs and into burial grounds. In the Old World, archaeologists have found cremation invariably associated with higher cultures. For example, cremation was the typical mode of burial of the late Bronze Age people of Europe. In North America, many of the later and highly developed Mound Builders cremated their dead. It is unlikely, therefore, that an early and simple hunting folk such as the earliest Americans should have disposed of their dead by cremation.

Also, cremation invariably leaves a residue of charred fragments. The Bronze Age people of Europe of 1600 B.C. used to bury these remains in urns. So also did the later Romans. But even if the cremated remains are discarded, the fragments of burned human bone are distinctive. A competent anthropologist can recognize one such tiny fragment and pronounce it human. Not only this, but a good physical anthropologist can tell you, from the examination of the joint surfaces of a few pieces of cremated bone, the age and sex of the individual they came from. Certain joint surfaces of the human body never quite stop growing and these surfaces reveal telltale evidences of the age of the individual. Sex differences are also evident to the anthropologist in the shape, size, or thickness of the bones involved. As no fragments of cremated human bone have ever been found on any camping place of early man in America, it is almost certain that they did not dispose of their dead in this way.

It has been suggested that the first Americans had mysterious burying grounds which have never been located. Others have argued that they placed their dead in caves or in crevices in the rocks. If so, these locations have never been found. It is far more likely that the first Americans did nothing at all with their dead, but let them lie where they fell.

Thirty thousand years ago, America was a dangerous

place. It is doubtful that anybody died a natural death asleep at camp. It is far more likely that the hunters, and perhaps their women and children also, met violent ends and probably at an early age. An early American hunter constantly risked death when trying to kill the great elephants of the Ice Age with a puny spear. Whole groups of early Americans might have perished crossing ice fields or have been killed by stampedes of wild animals. If we picture the hazards of that far-off time, it is amazing that these hardy people survived at all. But survive they did and we have found abundant evidences of their handiwork and of the camp sites where they squatted around fires to cook the meat of their kills.

A considerable part of the difficulty besetting the search for the skeleton of the first American is the result of early setbacks in this direction. During the first years of American archaeology in the nineteenth century, many people searched eagerly for the fossilized remains of men in the New World. When none was found, many scientists lost interest in the problem or became pessimistic. The skeletons which were discovered were identified as the remains of Indians "of only the last few hundred years or so." These finds were so identified because scientists were positive that any early type of human being would show primitive physical characteristics. It was thought that human beings existing in America 30,000 years ago must have been beetle-browed ape men. This idea, of course, leans upon discoveries in the Old World and especially in Europe.

In Europe, human skeletons were sometimes found with their artifacts. A whole series of very primitive human beings were found who were not at all like modern men. This whole family of beetle-brows was called the "Neanderthaloids" after the Neanderthal man who was the best known of the group. Even though, in most cases, the brains of these early men were just as large as those of modern man, their features and the contours of their heads were bestial and low-browed. Their bodies, also, were stooped and squat.

Quite naturally over a long period of years, European scientists had concluded that modern man descended from these low-brow ancestors and that transition had been made through intermediate forms of humanity not so primitive in appearance. With new discoveries, especially in the late 1930s and 1940s, it became evident that such a simple view of evolution was not correct. At several places, at Swanscombe in England, at Fontechevade in France, and at Kanjera in East Africa, human fossils of a very different type were discovered. These belonged to people of quite modern appearance, and yet were found among tools of very early Ice Age times. It became apparent that the family tree of man had contained at least two major kinds of ancestors. One of these was of apelike and primitive appearance and the other differed in no essential from people today. In Europe, then, and in other places in the Old World, a modern-appearing skull might not necessarily be of recent origin. A man of extremely modern appearance undoubtedly was the contemporary of the very primitive Neanderthal type. These modern-appearing men were called "Neanthropic." There is considerable evidence in Europe that Neanthropic man killed off his Neanderthal contemporary. At Krapina in Yugoslavia, archaeologists found a cave which contained the broken bones of Neanderthals. The Neanderthals had been killed and eaten.

However, even in the 1930s, many American scientists

clung to the old idea that what isn't primitive in appearance isn't ancient. The chief proponent of this theory was Dr. Aleš Hrdlička. Dr. Hrdlička was, for many years, chief anthropologist of the National Museum in Washington. Dr. Hrdlička, as the dean of physical anthropologists, passed upon all skeletal finds which were made in North and South America. He believed implicitly that the earliest type of American must have been primitive in skeletal feature. Many skulls were brought to Dr. Hrdlička for his opinion. If the skull was not bestial and low-browed, he immediately pronounced it of recent date and little value. It did not matter under what circumstances the skull was found, it was not old if it was not morphologically primitive. As one disappointed archaeologist expressed it, "Hrdlička stands like Horatio at the bridge, to prevent the entrance of modern man into America."

And Hrdlička did just that until his death in 1943. By that time, a number of the largest camping places of Folsom and Sandia man had already become excavated and publicized. The absence of human skeletons in these ancient places was no surprise to Dr. Hrdlička, who believed these were recent Indians anyway. But when presumably early skeletons were found, Hrdlička expected them to be Neanderthaloids. Actually, Dr. Hrdlička never fully believed that the earliest Americans had come to the New World as long ago as 30,000 years. When some skeletons were found which seemed to have claim to great antiquity, Hrdlička was not at all convinced.

One of the first finds to achieve nationwide publicity was called Calaveras Man. The Calaveras skull, made famous by Bret Harte's poem, was allegedly found in 1886, 130 feet below the surface in a mine at Bald Hill in Calaveras County, California. The find was made by J.

Whitney, a geologist, who discovered the skull embedded in earth layers laid down millions of years ago, even before the Ice Age. The skull was undoubtedly human and was of a type known as Cro-Magnon, the name of a mixture of Neanthropic men of Europe associated with the last of the Ice Age in France. If the Calaveras man was what he seemed to be, human beings must have existed earlier in America than in the Old World. Even Hrdlička was intrigued at first because the Calaveras skull showed some primitive characteristics.

Dr. Hrdlička examined the Calaveras cranium and wrote about it as late as 1907. The close scientific investigation to which this skull was subjected revealed that the Calaveras man was a fake. The state geologist who had first discovered the skull pulled it from the side of the mine shaft in good faith. But some of his friends had evidently thought it would be a great joke to plant a fossil skull in these early deposits. It was. The joke was so successful that none of the friends dared to admit the forgery after reams of paper had been consumed in learned scientific controversy and the skull had been given to Harvard University.

The Calaveras skull was not the only hoax perpetrated in the name of early man. The archaeological world was shocked to learn in 1953 of the undeniable proof that the famous Piltdown skull of England was a cleverly contrived fake. Chemical tests revealed that the skull and jaw had been artificially antiqued. Further chemical tests showed the bones to be modern. There have been a number of similar hoaxes of lesser importance in both North and South America. Fortunately most of these were discerned by astute archaeologists before news of them broke into print. Just as in a detective story there are false clues, these are to be expected in a mystery as important as that of the earliest American.

Even if we no longer contend, as Hrdlička did, that the inhabitants of America must have been primitive in appearance, the problem is still most disturbing. We don't know what to expect. Was the first American a Mongoloid? Or did he look different from later-day American Indians? Or perhaps the first American actually was a member of the Neanderthaloid tribe who came through Siberia in the early days and was the first to migrate to Alaska.

There have been several candidates for the honor of being the first Americans. Most have been discarded for one reason or another. The Lagoa Santa skeletons from southern Brazil have been identified as being quite modern because of evidence yielded by recent excavations. A skeleton found under New Orleans and another found near Natchez, Mississippi, were also eliminated because there was not enough evidence to establish their age.

One of the most disappointing of the discoveries purporting to be that of the first American was made in New Mexico not far from Sandia Cave. A human skull was excavated in 1926 from a cave in Bishops Cap Peak in southwestern New Mexico by paleontologists interested in the bones of extinct animals. The Bishops Cap Cave was full of bone beds of Ice Age animals of many fascinating sorts. According to the report, a human skull was found among these. But the paleontologists were so carried away by the large number of animal bones there that they failed to note carefully the location or the surroundings of the human skull. The human cranium itself was lost in shipment to California. In 1929, some years after the original excavations, Professor Kirk Bryan, the same Harvard geologist who worked on the Sandia Cave, attempted to evaluate the find because he had visited the excavations at Bishops Cap. His conclusions were unfortunately indecisive.

A flash in the pan was the discovery of a skeleton in 1935 only 14 miles from the original Folsom discovery at Dead Horse Gulch near Folsom, New Mexico. This skeleton was found deep in the bank of an arroyo under circumstances which seemed to indicate great antiquity. Dr. J. D. Figgins, the man who wrote of the original Folsom discovery, concluded at first that this skeleton was that of one of the very men who had killed the Ice Age bison at the Folsom site. He named the skeleton *Homo novusmundis,* or New World Man. But unfortunately further excavation at the site showed that although *Homo novusmundis* was indeed a New World Man, he wasn't very old. Apparently the skeleton was that of a fairly modern Indian who had been buried in a crack in the ground on the side of the arroyo. This was by no means the first American.

One of the most promising candidates for the honor of being the first American was found in Florida at Vero Beach, not far from Miami. Dr. E. H. Sellards of the Texas Memorial Museum in Austin, Texas, one of the paleontologists most concerned with this problem, made the find himself. In 1916 Dr. Sellards was digging in some mucky ground just behind the beach in which a number of skeletons of mammoths and mastodons had been discovered. Since Dr. Sellards was a paleontologist and a scientist, the digging was carried out very carefully so as to avoid any mistake. In addition, the human remains weren't lost and the circumstances of their discovery were carefully noted. Dr. Sellards and his co-workers found that three layers could be distinguished in their Vero Beach dig. The uppermost sand and muck of the first layer contained pottery and shell implements of recent Indians. Below this was another bed of sand in which the bones of extinct mammals were scattered and in which some human bones were found. A third stratum down was a marine deposit in which the diggers found no bones of animals or human beings.

The archaeologists were sure that human beings had lived at Vero Beach some time after the ocean waters which had covered it retreated. This took place during the last Ice Age when vast quantities of water vapor were locked up in the form of ice and the ocean levels were lowered. The presence of skeletons of mastodons and mammoths, both typical elephants of the Ice Age, fixed the time very closely. The human bones found in the same layer with those of the elephants semed to be of the same period. Dr. Sellards believed that these human bones were of Ice Age men, and certainly the skeletons of the first Americans. He was not dismayed to find that these human bones were not at all primitive in appearance. Indeed, the Vero man, as he came to be called, had a quite modern appearance.

Some ten years after the original discovery at Vero Beach, two other enthusiastic workers, James Gidley and Frederick Loomis, were digging in some very similar deposits near Melbourne, Florida, about 30 miles away. These two archaeologists also found pieces of human skeletons one layer down from the surface. In this second layer there were the bones of extinct Ice Age animals. Gidley and Loomis also were convinced of the contemporaneity of the human and the animal bones. They did, however, suggest that the whole complex might be of a somewhat later age. The Ice Age animals themselves may have lingered in the pleasant climate of Florida long after the Ice Age had come to a close in more northern regions.

For a number of years some archaeologists thought that the first Americans had been found. Large signs on the highway near Vero and Melbourne proclaimed to the casual tourist that he might, for the modest sum of 25 cents, view the actual remains of the first living American. The large painted picture which accompanied this announcement looked something like Tarzan of the Apes, but perhaps this aberration may be laid to advertising enthusiasm.

A number of archaeologists were not so sure that the Vero and Melbourne finds were really bones of Ice Age men. Dr. Irving Rouse, now of Yale University, announced in 1951 after considerable study that he did not think the human bones were deposited at the same time as those of the extinct animals. Rouse suggested that later Indians dug a hole, and disturbed an earlier burial in so doing. A few stone and bone tools found with the human bones were the same as those used by much later "archaic" people of Florida. There certainly is a possibility that the Florida skeletons may have ben interred from the present surface. Unfortunately, chemical analyses of the mineral content of the human and animal bones have been inconclusive. Analysis of the fluorine content, which would indicate the amount of fluorine the bones absorbed from the surrounding soil, also did not show incontrovertibly whether the human bones and those of the Ice Age animals were of the same age.

Most archaeologists, after carefully studying all the evidence at Vero and Melbourne, were at least skeptical. Of course, when Dr. Hrdlička examined the skulls, he did not find the primitive features which he always demanded as proof of antiquity. Other scholars were not so insistent upon a beetle-brow, but were still understandably reticent to point to the crushed skulls from Vero and Melbourne and say, "Undoubtedly there is an Ice Age American." Carbon 14 tests could not be made on the human bones themselves as they had not been burned. Unluckily, as long as any doubt remains, we cannot advance this human being to first place among the earliest Americans.

Another skeleton of a possible first American was found in Minnesota. This skeleton is of a female and is usually referred to by archaeologists as "Minnesota Minnie." Minnesota Minnie was discovered by some road laborers who were working on a highway just north of Pelican Rapids in Minnesota in 1931. While digging a road bed through a gravel terrace, they uncovered an almost complete skeleton about 10 feet below the surface. They also found two curios with the body, one a circular piece of shell, with two perforations by which it must have been hung around the neck of Minnesota Minnie as an ornament. The other was a dagger about 9 inches long made of a splinter of elk antler.

The workmen were intrigued by the fact that the skeleton lay at such a great depth below the surface. They carried their find in to Dr. A. E. Jenks of the University of Minnesota. Dr. Jenks immediately realized that this skeleton might well be that of the first American which archaeologists had been seeking.

Professor Jenks redug the glacial silts and layers of gravel where the workmen had found the body. He found other fragments of bone to indicate that the skeleton had actually lain in that position. And yet these silts and gravels had been laid down in the bed of a glacial lake which had been named Lake Pelican by geologists. No lake exists there today, although there is no doubt that such a body of water was present during the last of the Wisconsin glaciation. If Minnesota Minnie was buried in the glacial silt, there could be no doubt that she had been there during glacial times and had drowned or been thrown into the glacial lake when it existed. The layers of silt and gravel were just as strong proof of the date of this skeleton as any mammoth bones might be.

Minnesota Minnie proved to be a girl about fifteen years

old. Professor Jenks published a whole book about her. In it he pointed out that she had certainly been no beauty. Indeed, her teeth were so large and her face so protruding that this girl might have felt at home with any of the lower apes. Even the implacable Dr. Hrdlička was almost satisfied with the primitive character of Minnesota Minnie.

Dr. Hrdlička, true to his "Horatio at the Bridge" reputation, proclaimed that Minnesota Minnie was not an Ice Age woman at all but a modern Sioux Indian girl, albeit a very ugly one. Dr. Hrdlička pointed out that if this girl had been drowned in a Pleistocene lake, the body would have become disjointed and scattered about by the action of the waves. Another scientist, Dr. Ernst Antevs of Arizona, supported Dr. Hrdlička's contention, although on different grounds. Dr. Antevs also thought that later Sioux Indians had buried the girl in a small ravine or cleft in the glacial gravels in very recent times, which would account for the depth at which the workmen found the skeleton.

Professor Jenks replied vigorously to these contentions. He pointed out that the Minnesota girl was laid down among varve clays. These varve clays were formed in the bed of Lake Pelican shortly after the last major advance of the Wisconsin glaciation. The layers of varve clays and the gravels above them were undisturbed, argued Professor Jenks. How could any later Sioux Indians have buried one of their women so deeply? Besides, the thing didn't look like a Sioux burial. Dr. Antevs answered that there was no sure indication that this skeleton was of Ice Age date. Dr. Antevs even found a story recorded in reports of the nearby Sioux reservation which said that a girl of fifteen with an ugly face had been involved in a drinking brawl and murdered. She was buried secretly and by night. This might be the very girl.

And so the controversy raged. Many archaeologists said that Minnesota Minnie was. Others claimed just as determinedly that she wasn't. Professor Jenks, the discoverer of Minnie, definitely believed that Minnesota Minnie was an Ice Age individual.

In spite of earlier embarrassment over the fraud of the Calaveras skull, California has since produced two aspirants for first honors. One of these, called the Stanford skull, was discovered in 1922 by a Stanford University student. He found a human skull 20 feet below the surface of the bank of San Francisco Creek near Stanford, California, after a flash flood had poured down the creek bed and exposed it. The skull was embedded in hard-packed gravel and seemed by its very situation to be of considerable age. A geologist, who had worked closely with Hrdlička, announced cautiously that the Stanford skull might be as much as 4,000 years old.

Later scientists, looking at the Stanford skull in the light of more recent finds, were also impressed with its antiquity. Some thought that it might be much older than 4,000 years and might even represent the earliest American. Its physical makeup was like that of a modern California Indian. However, there was nothing to prove that the Stanford skull was not very ancient. Unfortunately, there were no tools or points with the skull by which it could be dated.

Los Angeles also lays claim to a "Los Angeles man." Actually there are two skulls which vie for the honor of representing the first Los Angeles resident. One find was that of a human skeleton dug up in 1914 from the La Brea tar pits just off Wilshire Boulevard. These tar pits are gummy and treacherous sink holes formed by the evaporation of natural oils. Apparently these tar pits are many thousands of years old. Excavators found the Los Angeles skeleton trapped in the black sticky stuff. Artifacts and tools found with the body were typical of later Californian times. Skeptics pointed out that a man trapped in the sticky tar might sink down in a few years to a level containing much older bones.

Another Los Angeles man was uncovered in 1936 while W.P.A. workmen were excavating a storm drain along the Los Angeles River. Thirteen feet below the surface the workmen found a human skull and some fragments of other bones. They continued digging at the side of the trench and uncovered the better part of a human skeleton. Scientists from the University of Southern California rushed to the scene to do some digging of their own. In the course of further excavations, a couple of bulky teeth of an Ice Age elephant were found not far away. Most of the scientists concluded that the Los Angeles skeleton was the first American. But there still was the shadow of a doubt that somehow this skeleton might have been buried from the surface at a later time. Anyway the skull was badly broken and little information could be derived from it.

Mexico also offered a skull as that of the first human being in the New World. This skeleton is called Tepexpan man because it was discovered in 1949 in the Valley of Mexico near the village of Tepexpan, where the Federal Insane Asylum is situated. Tepexpan man has the distinction of having been discovered by scientists in a scientific manner.

Dr. Hellmut deTerra, who has worked in paleolithic levels in both the Old World and the New, believed that most of the discoveries pertaining to the first American were worthless because they were first found by workmen or unskilled persons who destroyed most of the supporting evidence before archaeologists could arrive on the scene.

Consequently, together with Dr. Hans Lundberg, a geophysicist, Dr. deTerra acquired some World War II surplus mine detectors and went looking for early man. He decided to search in the Valley of Mexico and especially near the village of Tepexpan. Here, in laying water pipes, workmen had already encountered the skeletons of mammoth at a very shallow depth. Here the investigators, with their mine detectors, hoped to discover Ice Age man himself.

After several weeks of searching the surface with the electrically operated mine detectors, the investigators decided on four likely spots for digging, according to the buzzing of their machines. These spots were marked by stakes and the digging began. Three of the spots were only deposits of underground water. The fourth contained a human skeleton.

The skeleton lay face down. The knees were drawn up to the stomach. It looked as if the person had been killed in an ancient swamp and had fallen face down in the mud. Some of the bones of the back were missing as though scavenging animals, or perhaps vultures, had gnawed off parts while they were exposed.

Tepexpan man was widely heralded as the first indisputable find of an Ice Age American. Studies indicated that the skull had belonged to a man of about sixty years of age who had stood five feet seven inches tall. The skull showed no primitive characteristics such as would have delighted Dr. Hrdlička, but most archaeologists had come to expect that the first American would not necessarily be primitive at all.

Additional discoveries at the nearby site of Santa Isabel Istapán were those of projectile points and flake tools in association with the bones of mammoth. Other finds of tools of ancient men along with Ice Age mammals have added to the certainty that human beings were actually present in the Valley of Mexico during the last of the Wisconsin Period.

But alas for Tepexpan man and his crown of antiquity, two archaeologists, in a re-examination of the site, pointed out that the skeleton may have been buried in a pit dug from the surface. In their enthusiasm in excavating the original find, archaeologist deTerra and his friends were not careful enough in their digging. Perhaps the evidence of a pit from the surface dug by modern Indians existed and perhaps it did not. A faint shadow of doubt is enough. We are not quite sure whether Tepexpan man was an Ice Age American or a fairly modern Mexican Indian.

There is also a human skull from South America which has been advanced to candidacy for first honors. This skull was found in Ecuador in 1925 at a place called Punin. The discovery was made by a group of paleontologists who were excavating bones of extinct mammals. But as with the other skeletons, there is a shadow of doubt in the case of Punin man. The evidence of his great antiquity is not indisputable.

Of all the finds of supposedly first Americans, there is only one which is admitted by all to be indisputably ancient. Even this one leaves something to be desired since we are not quite sure which kind of early American he was. But that this skeleton is ancient, there can be no doubt.

This authentic first human being was discovered accidentally in Texas. An oil field worker, Keith Glascock, made the find in 1953 while he was looking for ancient artifacts on a ranch near Midland, Texas. In the bottom of a blowout scoured by the wind, Glascock found two spear points and fragments of human bone. With a rare show of care and reticence, Glascock did not pull out all the bones from the surrounding gray sand but brought in some scientists to do the digging. Dr. Alex Krieger and Dr. Fred Wendorf went to the Scharbauer Ranch where Glascock had found the bones, and dug. Krieger and Wendorf found more fragments of human bone, enough to reconstruct the better part of a human skull. They also found some more spear points near the bones. These were like Folsom points in shape but lacked the typical fluting of the classic Folsom points. They also found burned stones and the broken bones of Ice Age horses, antelope, and bison. There seemed no doubt that the man had died there at the same time as had the Ice Age animals. At least some of the points had belonged to this man. Certain of the animal bones were burned where the man had apparently cooked meat.

Like Minnesota Minnie, however, the Midland man turned out to be no man at all, but a woman. The skull was extraordinarily narrow but, other than this, showed no special differences from the skulls of modern Texan Indians. Chemical analysis made on the human bones showed that the fragments of skull were of the same age as those of the horse and bison. It seemed that the Midland woman had lived in what is now central Texas during Ice Age times.

Some of the other skeletal candidates were probably early Americans, too, but this can't be proved absolutely. There is even some doubt about the exact place of the Midland woman in the picture of the first Americans. Although classic Folsom points have been found on the Scharbauer Ranch, none were found in very close proximity to the body. Perhaps the Midland woman was a member of a tribe that came slightly later than Folsom times. We would very much like to have a skeleton of Sandia man. Or better still, from the Alaskan mucks, the body of one of the very first men to set foot on New World shores. Tomorrow, next month, or next year, we shall find this man. He may be discovered by a ditch digger, or an archaeologist. When he is found, our knowledge of early America and the first Americans will be greatly increased.

6

Corn on the Cob

THE DUST ROSE in suffocating clouds. The archaeologists wore dust masks which, in the murky light of the cave, made them look like pig-snouted monsters. But the workers did not seem to notice the penetrating dust. They dug steadily with trowels and whisk brooms. At the lower levels of a series of layers of dry grass and dirt, one of the excavators pulled a withered husk from the crumbling bank in front of him. The thing looked like the dried stalk of a large plant which had a pod on its stem. The archaeologist, Dr. Herbert Dick, gave a muffled cry through his dust mask. This shrunken piece of ancient vegetation might have been a golden treasure to judge from the way in which the other archaeologists crowded around to view it.

What archaeologist Dick had found in 1948 in the dusty levels of Bat Cave, New Mexico, was indeed a treasure, at least by scientific standards. This withered stalk and pod was one of the most important clues toward the solution of the major American mystery of all: Where and when did American agriculture begin?

Following the days of the hunters of Ice Age animals in the New World, there came a time of adjustment. At the end of the glacial period, when the large animals which had been characteristic of former times became extinct, big-game hunting was no longer possible. Indeed, had the earliest Americans been any less adaptable, they might have become extinct also. But we human beings are omnivorous. We can eat almost anything if we have to. In the difficult centuries following the end of the great Ice Age, the early Americans turned more and more to vegetable foods.

Even the early hunters had undoubtedly discovered that there were many roots, berries, and nuts which were edible. By a series of experiments, they must have discovered which varieties were nutritious, which poisonous, and which merely filling. During post-glacial times, small groups of early Americans lived by gathering these vegetable foods and hunting such small animals as they were able to trap or kill. During this period of adjustment, human beings came to rely more and more on plants.

The actual cultivation of these plants marks the beginning of a new era. Cultivation involves not only the artificial care of certain plants but also the changes produced in plants through man's purposeful activity. Actually, some original food gatherers might have had private berry patches which they protected from destruction or intrusion, and yet this was not true cultivation. When these early Americans realized that by taking the very best berries and planting them they could produce fruit of an improved kind, then they began agriculture in the truest sense.

Agriculture was discovered in the Old World, probably in the country which is now Iraq. In ancient Iraq or Mesopotamia the first plants cultivated or improved upon by early man were the grains, wheat, barley, and rye. The beginnings of agriculture in the New World almost certainly had nothing to do with these beginnings in Mesopotamia. For one thing, the grains—wheat, barley, and rye—do not appear in New World agriculture. Also, there was no physical means by which agricultural products from the Old World could have reached America. Certainly the cultivation of wheat did not spread northward into Siberia where wheat could not grow. We are certain, then, that clever minds hit upon the idea of growing plants and improving upon them independently here in America. Unfortunately, that is about all we are certain of.

When later European explorers came to American shores, they found the Indians here growing a plant called maize. Columbus found the Indians growing corn on all the islands of the West Indies and on the mainland of Central America. Diego, the brother of Columbus, reported that in one place he walked through an Indian corn field for 18 miles. This plant, Indian maize, the Europeans mistakenly called "corn." Actually the word "corn" means a kernel. Thus we have a "peppercorn" which is a kernel of pepper and "corned beef" which is beef prepared with corns or kernels of salt. To be correct, a diner in a restaurant should ask for "maize on the cob." However, the word "corn" is now embedded in usage as the name for the major agricultural product grown by the American Indians.

When the Europeans learned how to grow Indian corn from the original Americans, they found, to their astonishment, that the aborigines knew many varieties of corn. All agricultural Indian tribes were growing such different kinds as pod corn, sweet corn, dent corn, and flint corn. When the Hopi Pueblo Indians of northern Arizona were first seen by Spanish explorers, they knew and were cultivating over 80 varieties of corn. Such diversity would seem to indicate that the American Indians had been growing corn for a very long time.

The corn plant itself has come a very long way. Since the cobs grow directly on the side of the parent stalk, Indian corn has no way of spreading its own seeds. If the plant is untended by man, the mature cobs fall at the foot of the parent stalk. Then, if the kernels sprout in the succeeding season, they come up as a close-growing clump of shoots which crowd each other out. Ordinarily corn must be weeded and tended, and if planted too thickly it will not mature to produce cobs. If a stalk of corn is left untended by human hands, it will die out and fail to reproduce itself in two or three seasons at best. That is to say, corn in its developed state no longer can revert to the wild and has already been changed radically under the hand of man.

Corn also is a delicate plant. It is very susceptible to frost, and to various parasites. It cannot stand the competition of weeds. Corn requires at least 15 inches of annual rainfall to mature and flourishes only with a considerably greater amount of rainfall than that.

In looking for the point of origin of corn in the New World, archaeologists and botanists tried to keep all these considerations in mind. They could not look for the point of origin of corn in the northern part of North America or the extreme southern part of South America, where frosts would not permit corn to mature. The most obvious clue would lie in the discovery of some wild ancestor of corn from which clever early Americans could have derived the cultivated product of later times. Also, the most obvious place to look would be in civilized centers where corn had been cultivated for many centuries.

In looking for the place of origin, archaeologists focused their attention upon the Mayan area of southern Mexico and Guatemala. Here were abundant evidences of a very ancient civilization whose very existence depended upon the growing of maize. Botanists also focused their attention upon the Mayan area and were rewarded.

In the highlands of Guatemala, growing close by some of the ruins of the Mayan cities, they discovered a tall grassy plant called teosinte or teocentli. This plant bears only a superficial resemblance to corn, lacking the characteristic heavy stalk and cobs. Nevertheless, the botanists were able to demonstrate that teosinte is a relative of modern corn. For example, the two plants interpollinate if grown close together, so they are definitely related. The archaeologists were jubilant over this discovery. From the evidence contained in teosinte, it was obvious that the earliest ancestors of the Mayans had discovered the cultivation of teosinte and had cleverly developed it into the food plant of later days.

Easy explanations always seem doomed to error, especially when they deal with a subject as complex as human life. With further calculations, botanists realized that even with purposeful propagation it would take some 20,000 years to produce corn on the cob from teosinte. And when we speak of purposeful propagation, we have to presuppose a whole line of aboriginal Burbanks changing the plant from year to year with previous knowledge of the end product toward which they were striving. And even then there is considerable doubt as to whether teosinte could have been changed into food corn no matter how long it took or how it was manipulated by early man. It became evident that Indian corn did not come from teosinte. This revelation was especially embarrassing to many archaeologists, some of whom had named a professional publication *Teocentli* in honor of the original discovery.

In spite of the teosinte fiasco, most American archaeologists still felt that the point of origin of corn was somewhere in or near Central America. "Pod corn," which now grows in the northern part of South America, was thought by some botanists to be a possible original ancestor of modern corn.

Pod corn is characterized by the fact that each individual kernel is covered with six small husks. This arrangement is more typical of wild grasses than of ordinary maize, thus pod corn is closer in appearance to the wild corn from which all Indian corn is derived. If circumstances are favorable pod corn will grow wild for a few generations.

Excavator Herbert Dick's discovery in Bat Cave, New Mexico, in 1948 was a kind of pod corn. His findings at Bat Cave were augmented by the findings of a group of archaeologists from the Chicago Museum of Natural History in Tularosa Cave in New Mexico only two years later. Archaeological evidence in the American Southwest indicates that agriculture did not begin in New Mexico where both these caves are located. And yet in Bat Cave and Tularosa Cave fragments of cobs, grains, and stalks of a very primitive kind of pod corn were found mixed with other ancient debris in what seemed to be extremely old deposits. Radioactive carbon tests on the earliest of these corn fragments showed them to be 4,500 years old. The varieties of corn were closest to pod corn. Some very early people in what is now New Mexico were growing primitive varieties of Indian corn there over 4,000 years ago.

In the search for wild relatives of maize, some interesting ears of fossil corn turned up. On his famous voyage around the world, Charles Darwin found on San Lorenzo Island just off the Peruvian coast some corn cobs embedded in a marine deposit 85 feet above the present level of the sea. As this would imply, if taken at face value, that maize existed millions of years ago, a more ready explanation is probably the true one. The deposit which Darwin discovered on San Lorenzo Island was most probably the camping place of some Peruvian Indians of only a few hundred years ago. These later aborigines ate shellfish and corn on the cob and threw the refuse together on their garbage pile above the beach.

Far more intriguing was an ear of petrified corn which turned up in a curio shop in Cuzco, Peru, in 1920 and later found its way to the Smithsonian Institution. Many archaeologists and botanists examined this fossilized corn and decided that it was unquestionably a petrified ear of Indian maize. They were puzzled, however, by the fact that this interesting fossil, although ancient, was not primitive in structure. It was, as a matter of fact, almost identical with a cob of corn which one might buy in Cuzco today. The botanists finally decided that this valuable specimen should be sacrificed to extract the information its insides might contain. It was cut in two and found to be made of potter's clay. At its center was a hollow cavity containing three baked clay balls. Some clever Peruvian had long ago manufactured the "petrified" ear of corn as a rattle for his baby.

Many other reports of wild corn, or near-wild corn, have turned out to be maize crossed with teosinte with which it will readily interpollinate. Burbank himself, when his reputation for purposefully breeding some dozens of food plants into various forms was at its height, decided to solve the mystery of the origin of maize. He started with teosinte and, after eighteen generations of skillful breeding of the plant, produced a passable but primitive variety of maize. He later discovered, to his chagrin, that he had not started with teosinte at all, but had begun his experiments with a hybrid of teosinte and maize. Even the great Burbank died without solving the mystery.

Thus, the family tree of maize, with its unusual and baffling cobs and kernels, continues to elude detection. There is no doubt that the root of the tree is the root of all the great New World civilizations. Without the development of maize, the great cultures of America would have been impossible.

But Indian corn was not the only plant upon which agriculture in the New World was based. Reaching back into antiquity in the same manner as maize are the two vegetables, the bean and squash. New World beans, a vine product, appear extremely early and were, in most agricultural communities, almost equal in importance to maize. The bean provides protein, forming a substitute for meat. Agricultural people usually have little time for hunting. With the cultivation of the bean, hunting was no longer necessary. It will be remembered that beans were also discovered and cultivated in the Old World. The commonest Old World beans are now often referred to as "navy beans," as they later served in a dried state as stores in the British Navy. New World beans are often called "pinto beans" because several varieties are painted or mottled in color. The Old World beans and the New World beans were cultivated separately by the earliest Old World and New World farmers.

Squashes and pumpkins were undoubtedly found growing wild by the early inhabitants of America and were cultivated. Various groups of American Indians still grow distinct kinds of pumpkins and squashes. These varieties are kept separated and intact by the careful selection of seeds of individual fruits. The individual species will readily merge again if planted close enough together to allow the pollen grains to mix. Pumpkins and squashes, if cultivated within a few feet of each other, will produce "squmpkins," or pumpkins with warts. The form of the vine from which all squashes and pumpkins was orginally derived has changed little from the wild state.

In most North American cultures, corn, beans, and squash formed a sacred trinity. It was for many the basic agricultural combination. The Pueblo Indians of the American Southwest, for example, regarded the gods of corn, bean, and squash as the three major ruling deities.

In the Andean area of South America, a major center of agricultural development appeared in very early times. Some archaeologists believed that all agricultural products, including maize itself, originated in what is now Peru. Agricultural products there have been traced back to at least 2,000 years before Christ. In this area appeared so-called Irish potatoes, pineapples, peanuts, lima beans, kidney beans, peppers, and tomatoes.

The potato, called Irish because it was later grown in Ireland, was originally a plant of the moist mountain valleys of Peru. It was cultivated by the early people there for the starchy tubers that accumulate on its roots. Today, the Andean potato is a plant which makes life possible in many parts of the world. It was brought to Europe from Peru in 1585 and is today the basic food supply of several European countries.

The lima bean, named from ancient Lima, Peru, was grown in prehistoric times in several varieties. The ancient Andeans, especially, liked a very large version of the lima bean which they not only ate but also used as a medium for the writing of messages. A messenger often carried an inscribed lima bean for hundreds of miles along mountain trails.

The peanut, also a root plant, is not a nut at all. The peanut was an important source of protein and oils, so necessary to a people who no longer hunted wild animals. The ancient Peruvians often made pottery replicas of peanuts, potatoes, lima beans, and other agricultural products with which they were familiar. These replicas show that the forms of these plants were essentially the same many centuries ago as they are today. Of course, modern gardeners have, with careful selective breeding and modern methods, brought all these New World products to peaks of perfection. But their origins are known and their form has not changed essentially.

The sweet potato, which also appears in ancient South America, presents a more difficult archaeological problem. Apparently the sweet potato, a relative of the morning glory, originated in tropical South America. It was grown by the Andeans and also by many of the earliest people of the Amazon Basin and other parts of tropical South and Central America. At some time in antiquity, the sweet potato was carried westward to the islands of the Pacific. When the Hawaiian Islands were first discovered by Europeans, the Hawaiians were growing sweet potatoes. Other islands in the mid-Pacific also knew the sweet potato. The introduction of this one cultivated plant, apparently from America, is the more mysterious because other American plants did not appear. Maize, demonstrably the most ancient and important of American plants, was not carried to the Pacific islands and yet maize grows very well under tropical and semitropical conditions.

In this connection, an archaeological mystery has appeared in southeastern Asia. Chinese literature, and also the folklore of Burma, contains descriptions of plants which sound like Indian corn. More than fifty years ago, a missionary in western China found primitive villagers growing Indian corn. Primitive agricultural people in the hill country of Assam and Burma also grow kinds of corn which can be ground into meal as well as a variety for parching and popping. When questioned about this, both the Chinese and the Burmese stated that they had grown corn from time immemorial. Some anthropologists, following the trail of the sweet potato, were certain that Indian corn from America had reached Asia thousands of years ago. Others have reversed this chain of evidence and suggested that Indian corn originated in Asia and therefore should be called Asiatic corn. The difficulty is, of course, that no maize appeared in any of the Pacific islands along with the sweet potato.

New World farmers of long ago also tried every kind of food tree which might serve their purposes. They ate all the wild fruits and nuts, and even, upon occasion, the bark of trees. The Indians of ancient America, however, contributed only one fruit tree to the present-day world. This was the avocado, probably first grown in the tropical regions of Central or South America.

In their search for food plants, the New World aborigines hit upon one which certainly does not supply food but is of great importance to many. This plant was tobacco. Tobacco was known and grown by all American Indian farmers who practiced agriculture. Tobacco was even cultivated by some Indian tribes who did not raise corn or any other farm products. Tobacco was one of the first American agricultural products to reach Europe and from there to circle the world. The use of tobacco spread faster than that of any of the food plants.

The agricultural contributions of the New World are

important and certainly equal those of Africa, the Near East, and China. Today, whole tribes of Africans and the people of countries in Europe and Asia subsist upon Indian corn, even though they may never have heard of an American Indian. Peanuts and Andean potatoes are basic foods for vast populations of Africa and Europe.

In the Old World, the great civilizations were based on agriculture and animal husbandry. What of the domestication of animals in ancient America? As far as we know, there weren't any domestic animals or birds in ancient America. Of course, we must note that after the Ice Age in America there were relatively few animals which would have been appropriate for domestication. But even at that, the early Americans were very behindhand in raising animals or birds for food or labor purposes.

In the Andean area, the llama was domesticated by the prehistoric Peruvians. The llama, and such wild relatives as the alpaca, the vicuña, and the guanaco are descendants of Ice Age camels. The camel became extinct in North America at the end of the Pleistocene Period. In South America these slightly built, long-necked camels lingered on. But the llama is not very useful as a domestic animal. It cannot pull heavy loads and it can carry only a small burden upon its back. Furthermore, llamas are intractable and difficult to care for. As sources of meat and milk they are of little importance. Llama hair can be turned into yarns, but the finer-textured hair of the wild vicuña and alpaca is better for this purpose. Men in the mountains of Peru can lift heavier weights and carry them greater distances than can the llamas.

The guinea pig was domesticated for food by the Andeans; but, judging from ancient replicas of these little rodents, even the early Peruvians were not enthusiastic about eating this kind of flesh, probably because of the repulsive smell. The guinea pig has now found his place as an experimental laboratory animal and thus is endeared to science. The Muscovy duck was also raised in captivity as were a few monkeys and bright-plumed birds.

In Central America and North America, there were even fewer domestic animals and birds than in South America. The prehistoric Mexicans and Mayas kept parrots and quetzals in order to harvest their bright-colored feathers. The Pueblos of the American Southwest domesticated the wild turkey. The turkey is a valuable domestic fowl and has a considerable amount of meat on his frame when adequately nourished. But the Pueblo Indians didn't raise turkeys for their meat. The turkey was a sacred bird to them. Its feathers were in great demand for the manufacture of prayer plumes. In most cases, it would seem, the Pueblo Indians kept turkeys for their feathers rather than their flesh.

In early America, the beginnings of civilization were based almost entirely upon agriculture. All the important domesticated animals and birds we now raise came from the Old World. Nevertheless, the New World farmers of long ago built a number of civilizations equal in accomplishments and scope to any of the Old World. American agriculture seems to have begun with maize. As each group of ancient Americans received the blessings of maize, their culture grew accordingly. The Indians used this plant as money, fuel, jewelry, building material, and for brewing beer. The civilizations which reached the highest level of attainment were those which practiced, over the longest period of time, the cultivation of maize, beans, and squash. The greatness of the achievements of ancient Americans is measured by corn on the cob.

7

The Mystery of the Mounds

BEFORE Thomas Jefferson became president of the United States, he was one of its first archaeologists. President Jefferson shared his interest in antiquity and past peoples with a number of educated men of his time. Americans of that day were not yet aware of the earliest backgrounds of the New World. They did not yet know the story of the migrations across the Bering Strait. Jefferson and his colleagues had never heard of Folsom man or concerned themselves with the problem of finding the skeleton of the first American.

President Jefferson was intrigued, though, by a mystery connected with earthen mounds which European settlers had found scattered from the St. Lawrence River Valley in the north to the southern tip of Florida. As the American colonists pushed farther and farther inland, they found more of these "tumuli" or "barrows," as they called them.

As the new colonists crossed the Appalachian Mountains and went into the valley of the Ohio River, they found thousands of these earthen mounds, some of which were of tremendous size. At this early stage in American archaeology, there was only one archaeological mystery. This was the mystery of the mounds.

After the War of Independence, Thomas Jefferson, perhaps for relaxation from his arduous civil duties, turned to the examination of this mystery which had interested him since his youth. Jefferson was not only one of the leading theorists about mounds and Mound Builders, but he was the first to dig and to record his digging as archaeological proof of his ideas. In a most interesting volume, *Notes on Virginia,* written about 1781 and published in 1801, Jefferson described the mounds of his native Virginia. He dug one of these, as he says, to learn who the Mound Builders were and to discover the purpose for which they had built the mound.

Jefferson writes in *Notes on Virginia* of a mound about 12 feet high in the valley of the Rivanna River: "I first dug superficially in several parts of it and came to collections of human bones, at different depths, from six inches to three feet below the surface . . . I conjectured that in this barrow might have been a thousand skeletons . . . Appearances certainly indicate that it has derived both origin and growth from the accustomary collection of bones and deposition of them together . . ."

Jefferson, with good scientific reasoning, attributed the burial mound to Indian tribesmen. Many archaeologists long after President Jefferson's day did not come as close to the truth as this. Jefferson further speculated that America may have been populated by Indians coming to Labrador by way of Greenland and Iceland or migrating to these shores from the Kamchatka Peninsula of Siberia or by way of Bering Strait. He finally concluded that they probably came by way of Bering Strait from northeastern Asia. This is an astounding deduction as, in Jefferson's day, most scientists were not aware that human beings had not originated in the New World. Most European and American scholars had concluded that the Garden of Eden, and consequently the point of origin of man, had been in the Holy Land. Nonetheless, Jefferson, as he speculated on the large number of Indian languages in America, concluded that the tremendous diversity of New World tongues showed that the Indians of America were a more ancient people than those of Asia. Later, when Thomas Jefferson became President of the United States, his interest in the mystery of the Mound Builders continued as did his speculations about their origins and ultimate fate.

Thomas Jefferson was not the only president of the United States who was interested in the mounds. General Washington, at about the time that Jefferson was digging his mound in Virginia, wrote in a letter to General Baker that he hoped the ancient mounds would give up their secret. But it was President William Henry Harrison who turned archaeologist and author to try to solve the Mound Builder mystery. Harrison wrote a book entitled, *Discourse on the Aborigines of the Valley of the Ohio,*" in which he posed a number of questions and attempted to answer them. The disappearance of the Mound Builders seemed to bother him more than the question of their origin. "If they had been made to yield to a more numerous or more gallant people, what country received the fugitives? And what has become of the conquerors?" Harrison had a theory about the origin of the builders of the mounds. He wrote: "The pictural records of that nation ascribe their origin to the Astecks, a people who are said to have arrived in Mexico about the middle of the seventh century. An

American author, the Rt. Rev. Bishop Madison of Virginia, having with much labor investigated this subject, declares his conviction that these Astecks are one and the same people with those who once inhabited the valley of the Ohio. The probabilities are certainly in favor of this opinion." Harrison, like Jefferson, came remarkably close to the truth in these romantic speculations.

While Thomas Jefferson's curiosity and William Henry Harrison's theories were leading them close to hidden truths, a large number of other Americans were also busy on the problem. Hundreds of farmers and amateur archaeologists were busy digging some thousands of mounds from Maine to Georgia. Few if any scientific results were ever obtained from these diggings. Large numbers of "Indian relics" did end up in the glass cases of historical societies, but these tools of a bygone age conveyed very little information. Most of the collectors, if they were concerned with the mystery of the mounds, considered it an unfathomable problem. But many governors of states, members of Congress, and scholars in American universities wrote about and wrestled with this mystery.

Up to the time of the Civil War, very little progress had been made in determining who had built the mounds or what they were for.

A number of European archaeologists had traveled through eastern America to look at the mounds and to make collections of Mound Builder relics. None could offer any help based on discoveries made in Europe. A faint connection was noticed with certain ancient Europeans of the Bronze Age who had buried their dead and built mounds of earth or stone over the graves. Classical scholars pointed out that Achilles of Trojan War fame had heaped a mound over the dead body of his friend Patroclus. Some of the American Mound Builders had obviously had metal tools, but there the analogy seemed to end. Mound Builders of the Ohio Valley used copper instead of bronze, and the bronze workers of Europe had different precedents and different descendants. No connection between European archaeology and the American Mound Builders could be proven.

Instead, most scholars fell back on the supposition that the American Mound Builders were descendants of the ancient Babylonians or Egyptians or some other Old World culture. A favorite theory during the early 1800s was that the Mound Builders were the descendants of the Ten Lost Tribes of Israel. These Ten Lost Tribes, it was pointed out quite scientifically, were at about the same level of development displayed by the works of the Mound Builders. A learned paper of 1805 written by the Rev. Thaddeus Harris of Massachusetts argues quite convincingly that the later American Indians could not have been descended from the Lost Tribes of Israel but that the builders of the mounds certainly were the offspring of the Lost Israelites. The author does not explain how the Ten Lost Tribes, driven out of Mesopotamia by the wicked King Sargon, got to the east coast of America.

All the early theories concerning the mystery of the mounds were long on guesswork and short on facts. Thomas Jefferson's excavation on his Virginia farm was probably the most scientific one for the next fifty years. Very little scientific digging whatsoever was carried on in the nineteenth century, although a lot of dirt was moved by a lot of people. Most of the century was devoted to collecting. It became known that these mounds of earth contained relics. Certain kinds of mounds contained better "loot" than others, and so diggers for pleasure or for profit learned where the best diggings might be found and dug there.

Collecting for the sake of collections is not peculiar to archaeology. At one time or another in the history of the world human beings have collected almost everything. There are certain rules to guide any collector. For one thing, a collection must be complete so as to outdo similar collections made by competitors. Most important of all, the rarer an item and the more difficult its acquisition, the greater its value in a collection. Whether you are collecting human heads or postage stamps, the rules are almost the same.

Collectors of Indian relics followed the rules implicitly. They dug mounds themselves and they subsidized farmers and laborers to dig for them. Collections of Indian relics numbering tens of thousands were amassed in this way. Seldom did it occur to any of these collectors to acquire information along with the relics. The things themselves were of intrinsic value. Any information which might have accompanied the relics was at first irretrievably lost as collections were handed down from father to son or purchased by some wealthy collector. Some dealers in antiquities actually went out of their way to obscure information about the origins of the objects in which they dealt. Sources were kept secret so that more digging could be done. The activities of dealers in Indian relics at about the time of the Civil War were widespread and involved all kinds of items. Men who bought and sold Indian relics came to be as common in New York, Philadelphia, New Orleans, and other large centers as traders in European lace or French wine, and the amounts of money involved were considerable. The popularity of Indian collecting in the middle of the nineteenth century may be ascribed not only to the collecting instincts of all men but also to the added interest in antiquity. The relics which connoisseurs eagerly sought and paid for had been made by a mysterious people who had lived long before the red Indians.

There were outstanding individuals among these collectors. One of the most famous was a wealthy eccentric named Cyrus Moore, who had made his money in cotton. With plenty of wealth at his disposal, he dedicated his whole life to digging mounds and acquiring the treasures which they contained. Every winter Moore had a houseboat built to order either at Cincinnati or St. Louis. When it was finished, he moved aboard and spent the ensuing summer drifting along the waters of the Ohio or Mississippi River with a crew of men. He carried twenty-five expert diggers. Since there were thousands of mounds along the Mississippi Valley and its tributaries, the diggers never lacked for sites for their busy shovels. As the houseboat was towed from place to place, several mounds might be excavated at once. The archaeological loot was quickly shaken out of the earth and brought onto the houseboat. It is recorded that Moore himself sat on the afterdeck of the houseboat in a special chair and played his banjo. Visitors to the floating museum could tell by the liveliness of the tune whether the excavators were finding rare items or just run-of-the-mill relics. Each fall the houseboat, with its tired but happy diggers aboard, pulled in to New Orleans full of Mound Builder treasures such as would make any other collector of the time green with envy. The next spring, the whole crew traveled north to take over another houseboat and repeat the process.

Collectors and collecting of this sort were not rare during the latter part of the nineteenth century. Inevitably, enormous accumulations of the relics got into the antiquarian societies and museums of the day. A great many were taken to Europe. It was from such collections rather than from the mounds themselves that certain archaeologists began to gather some information. But first some obvious questions came to the fore. The first was one which had been asked by every amateur digger and collector: "Who were the Mound Builders?"

It seemed obvious that they were not Indians, or at least not ordinary Indians. The Red Man with whom George Washington was familiar did not build mounds. Nor did any of the Shawnee or Iroquois or other tribes with which the early settlers were familiar. Not only that, but the modern Indians disclaimed any knowledge of the ancients who built the mounds. Indian tribes first encountered by Europeans had no knowledge of metal and yet some of the mounds were rich in metal tools and ornaments. It was pointed out, too, that for the building of the larger mounds, a highly organized society would have been necessary. None of the modern Indians, when they were first seen by Europeans, had the requisite degree of civilization.

Another question posed by the early collectors was: "How old were the mounds?" Obviously the Mound Builders had lived in the Mississippi and Ohio valleys a very long time before, since the modern Indians had forgotten them. Also, great trees, some of which were obviously hundreds of years old, were growing atop some of the mounds, indicating that the mounds must have been built before the trees took root.

The most discerning among the early archaeologists, such as General Rufus Putnam of the Ohio Company, asked the question: "Are all of the Mound Builders the same people?" Even the earliest collectors had noticed that there were several kinds of mounds. There were single mounds, and mounds in groups. There were round-topped mounds and flat-topped mounds both large and small. Also, the mounds had different kinds of things in and around them. Some of the mounds contained metal objects. Others disclosed marvelously carved stone pipes or other objects of art. Pottery found in mounds varied from place to place.

And the most consuming question of all concerned the fate of these people. If the Mound Builders were not ordinary Indians—and they did not seem to be—then where had they gone? How could a civilized metal-working people disappear to be replaced by primitive savages?

The first attempts to answer these and many other questions about the mysterious Mound Builders were made through studies of the collections of Indian relics. One of the first investigators, Charles Willoughby, spent his life studying the vast collections of the Peabody Museum of Harvard University, of which he was director. After many years of study, Dr. Willoughby wrote a book called *Antiquities of New England,* finally published in 1935, based upon his observation of thousands of Indian relics belonging to the museum and to private collectors in the East. By dividing these tools, weapons, and ornaments into various categories, Dr. Willoughby tried to discover who the Mound Builders were and to distinguish various tribes and time periods. He even attempted to guess what languages they spoke. In general he discovered very little.

One of the greatest collectors was Gerard Fowke, a Union cavalry officer during the Civil War. Even before the War between the States, Gerard Fowke had been a collector. By 1880, Fowke had probably seen and handled more Indian relics than had any other living man. He had visited and tabulated the collections of hundreds of local enthusiasts from Georgia to Michigan. An interesting thing about Fowke's investigation is that he traveled on foot. Fowke distrusted trains, especially after he was in a minor accident in one during the Civil War, and he swore when the war ended that he would never mount a horse again. He was as good as his word. Even when the newfangled horseless carriages began to scoot around the country roads with lightning speed, Fowke would have none of them. He considered walking to be the most dignified and surest mode of locomotion. He thought nothing of walking from Nashville, Tennessee, to Louisville, Kentucky, to see a new collection or to view a group of mounds which he had not visited before. Even as late as the 1920s Fowke's tall figure was a familiar sight on roads in Ohio, Indiana, and Illinois. He always wore leather cavalry boots which reached above his knees, scarcely ideal hiking equipment.

Covering thousands of miles in these antiquarian peregrinations, Fowke learned one thing. He found out that there were different kinds of mounds and different kinds of Mound Builders, many of whom could be recognized by the stone tools and ornaments they had left behind. Fowke also judged that some of the ancient people living east of the Mississippi had not built mounds at all.

By examining the many kinds of relics with which he was familiar, Fowke was able to divide them into categories. He concluded that the richest and most interesting objects came from Ohio; in fact, the Ohio River Valley was the richest collecting ground anywhere in the United States. Many of the objects found there were made of copper. There was also carved stone, of an artistic attainment unparalleled in any other place. During the last years of his walking tours, Fowke concentrated his studies in the Ohio area. He finally wrote a book, called *Archaeological History of Ohio,* in which he speculated as to whether the Mound Builders were Aztecs or Nahuas and quoted different authorities concerning the route which the earliest American colonists used to come to the New World. Fowke also catalogued in his book all previous knowledge of mounds and Mound Builders and listed all the different kinds of relics according to the categories into which he had divided them.

But even Gerard Fowke never realized the full complexity of the Mound Builder problem. Nor did the collectors, or those who studied collections, ever solve the mystery of the mounds. The real solution to the mystery lay in the earthen monuments themselves rather than in the objects entombed within them.

Just prior to the Civil War two men, one a surveyor and the other a lawyer, really began American archaeology. These two, who always worked together, were E. G. Squier and E. H. Davis. Squier and Davis had been for some years working in the Ohio River Valley surveying lands there and laying out farms. In their surveying activities, Squier and Davies had traveled as far west as Wisconsin and the Upper Mississippi Valley. They found thousands of earthen mounds scattered throughout the area but especially in the level river bottoms where the best farming lands lay. As Squier and Davis marked out their lines with their crude surveying apparatus, they discovered that most of the mounds they came upon were not simply tumuli or barrows such as those in Pennsylvania and Virginia. Many of the mounds of the Ohio River Valley were built in groups. The earthen embankments forming these groups were often built in circles, squares, hexagons, and other geometric figures. Round mounds and elongated mounds accompanied the geometric "works," as Squier and Davis called them. The two surveyors became so interested that they spent less and less time laying out farm fences and more and more time mapping and drawing ancient earthworks from Pennsylvania to Wisconsin. Ultimately their survey carried them down the Mississippi, where they mapped and pictured most of the important mound building centers of the lower Mississippi Valley. Squier and Davis also called upon local collectors of mound relics and used their maps as well as their own.

In 1848, Squier and Davis published the results of their survey in a work which was the first classic of American archaeology. *Ancient Monuments of the Mississippi Valley* was published by the Smithsonian Institution as the first volume of a series. With the appearance of this book, which is now a collector's item, Squier and Davis outlined for the first time the great mystery of the mounds. Most of the collectors who had been concerned with Indian relics had never realized the scope of the problem. A beaten copper breastplate was a wonder in itself. But what of a mound which required the labor of 100,000 men over perhaps twenty years to complete? *Ancient Monuments of the Mississippi Valley* made Americans and Europeans aware of this major mystery of antiquity. The Mound Builders had been as important in their day as the Egyptians or Mesopotamians in theirs. However, Squier and Davis propounded very naive theories as to who the Mound Builders were or where they had gone.

Squier and Davis surveyed much of the mound area and pointed out the immensity of the mound problem, but this was not all. They also excavated in some of the Mound Builder groups after they had finished their surveys. By modern archaeological standards, their digging was abominable and destructive. Present-day archaeologists would call such activity a "potato dig." Nonetheless, many modern archaeologists in the mound area would like to know what magical formula Squier and Davis used in their potato digging. Inevitably, and often after only a day or two of labor in one place in one mound of a large group of earthworks, Squier and Davis hit the most important deposit. In most of the ceremonial geometric works, especially in the Ohio River Valley, the ancient builders had left a cache of beautifully wrought objects in one place as an offering. This ceremonial cache usually consisted of tobacco pipes carved in the images of birds, animals, turtles, or fish. There were copper breastplates and copper headdresses, copper axes, bracelets, ear spools, and other ornaments. These ceremonial caches contained the highest artistic attainment of which the builders of the mounds were capable. All this they left in a deposit as an offering to their gods and their dead.

Squier and Davis amassed a collection of thousands of specimens comprising the finest objects the Mound Builders had to offer. They tried to sell this collection to an institution in the United States which would pay them enough to reimburse them for their expenses in the field. They were unsuccessful and the collection was purchased for the Blackmore Museum of Salisbury England. It now reposes in the British Museum.

Due to the efforts of Squier and Davis and also to those of the many students of collections of Indian relics, the United States government at last became interested in the mystery of the mounds. The Bureau of American Ethnology of the Smithsonian Institution began to act officially. Under the direction of Dr. Cyrus Thomas of the bureau, a survey of the entire mound area was started in 1880. Every state east of the Mississippi and a few west of the Mississippi were visited during the next ten years. Cyrus Thomas proved to be a dynamo of energy. He conducted most of these explorations personally. Even minor mounds in out-of-the-way stream valleys were placed on the official maps. Some digging was done, but for the most part the survey was an over-all attempt to outline the whole complex. Even Dr. Thomas was astounded at the results.

The official results of this first great survey were published in the twelfth annual report of the Bureau of American Ethnology in 1890. Cyrus Thomas and his associates had accomplished a Herculean task in ten years. We know that they located and placed on their maps less than half the mounds and earthworks which are now known to exist. Nevertheless, the immensity of the mound problem became known for the first time. Mounds of different sorts were found from Ontario, Canada, to the Gulf Coast of Florida, Mississippi, and Louisiana. Vast numbers of mounds, whose existence the early investigators had not suspected, were found in the valleys of the rivers west of the Mississippi. North Dakota, South Dakota, Nebraska, Kansas, Oklahoma, and eastern Texas were dotted by the works of the ancient Mound Builders. The government surveyors estimated that there were over a million mounds in the whole area. We now know that this estimate was conservative.

Many investigators tried to estimate in man-hours the labor necessary for the heaping up of all of the earth. Even the most modest estimates involved tens of thousands of people working for hundreds of years. We know that the mounds were built without the use of wheeled vehicles or the labor of draft animals. Both the wheel and domestic animals which could be used for traction were missing in ancient America. The mounds were piled up by the labor of many people bringing earth in baskets, sometimes from a long distance.

Imagine how many basket loads were necessary to pile up the Cahokia Mound which lies in the valley of the Mississippi River in East St. Louis. The main mound of the Cahokia group is a flat-topped truncated pyramid 1,080 feet long, 710 feet wide, and 100 feet high. In the group of mounds at Cahokia, there were originally 300 earthen piles of somewhat lesser size. The immensity of the physical labor involved amazes us, even in this day of bulldozers and monster earth-movers, and the degree of organization of the people who accomplished this work must have been equal to that of the builders of the pyramids of Egypt.

The activities of the Mound Builders obviously spread wide over North America. The early investigators had also shown that there were many kinds of Mound Builders building different sorts of mounds in this vast area. But in their trading activities these ancient people had gone far from the mounds which they built. In the collections of New England and among the ceremonial objects which Gerard Fowke described and which Squier and Davis found in the geometric works were many things which had been brought from places far beyond the frontiers of the mound area.

Of greatest interest was the metal which some of the Mound Builders habitually worked. Although they occasionally used gold nuggets and even a bit of silver, their commonest material was copper. Copper in an almost pure state came from deposits in the Isle Royal region of Michigan. It was this copper which led many earlier writers to suppose that the Mound Builders were connected with the metal-using Bronze Age people of Europe, or the bronze-smelting cultures of Mesopotamia. Actually, the American Mound Builders never made bronze, although much of their copper was accidently adulterated with other substances. The Mound Builders pounded the copper nuggets cold. They heated the copper as they worked it so that the metal would not become too crystalline and crack; but this process, known as annealing, is not true smelting. The American Mound Builders used copper more as a malleable stone than as a metal.

Remarkable are the channels of trade by which the mound-building peoples acquired the copper. Certain of the mound groups had much more copper than others. Copper was traded from Lake Superior to the Gulf of

Mexico; and shells from the Gulf region, especially the large conch shells of Gulf Coast waters, were traded up into Ohio and Illinois. Also from the south, groups of Mound Builders passed on alligator teeth, fossil shark teeth, and barracuda jaws, which must have been very valuable items by the time they reached the valley of the Ohio.

From the Far West, from the area which is now New Mexico, or perhaps from Wyoming, mound-building traders acquired obsidian, or black volcanic glass, which they chipped into beautiful sacrificial knives. Grizzly-bear teeth were also acquired by trade from the Rocky Mountain area. Mound-building people on the East Coast supplied sheets of silvery mica from the Carolinas and shells from the Atlantic shore. Stones which could be carried easily or which had a beautiful luster were traded from Connecticut and New Jersey to Illinois and Iowa.

In the inland streams, many of the mound-building people collected fresh-water clams. They used the shells for spoons and hoes. Occasionally they found a fresh-water pearl. These were considered treasures. A string of evenly matched pearls was as valuable to a Mound Builder chief as it was to any Far Eastern nabob. In certain ceremonial deposits which the Mound Builders left to their dead, gallons of fresh-water pearls have been recovered by archaeologists. The Ohio State Museum now keeps in its big safe several strings of these ancient pearls which still retain their luster. Some of these strings are valued at several thousands of dollars each.

With additional information of this kind, the mystery of the mounds deepened. Who were the people who had spread their activities over three-quarters of a continent? Were the Mound Builders indeed related to the Aztecs, as President Harrison had thought? How ancient were they?

Were they the ancestors of modern Indians? If so, why didn't modern Indians build mounds and work metal? Where did the Mound Builders fit into the scheme of ancient America? What language did they speak? What were they like in appearance?

These and a hundred other questions were asked by everyone who read Squier and Davis's book, *Ancient Monuments of the Mississippi Valley.* To answer these questions, archaeologists of the Bureau of American Ethnology began to dig. The mystery of the mounds could be solved only with the shovel. It was to bc fifty years and many millions of shovelsful later that the mystery was solved.

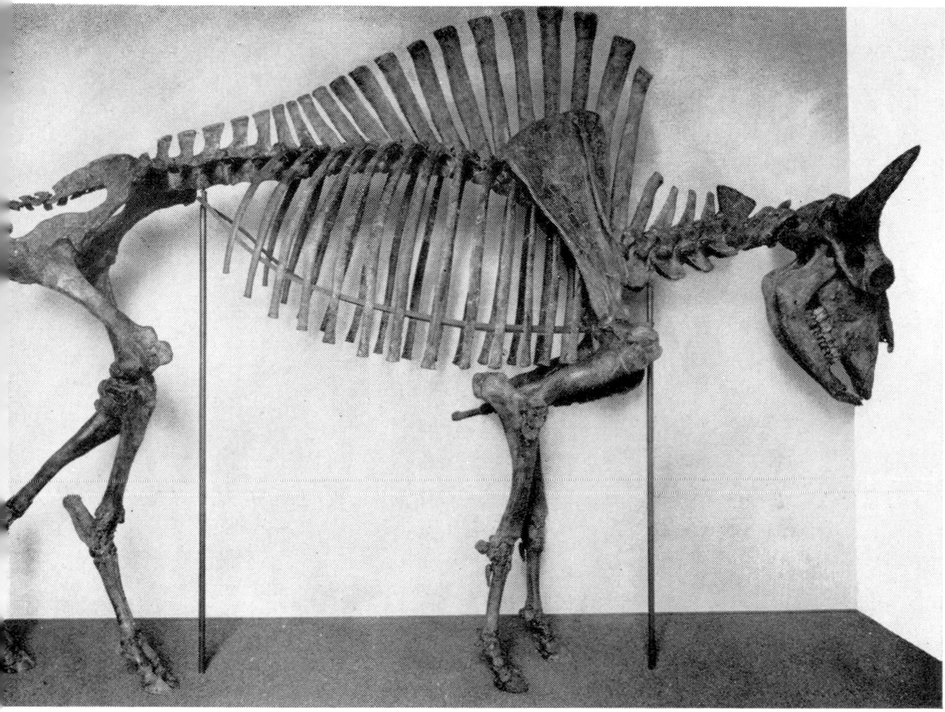

Plate 1. Mounted skeleton of Bison taylori, *the bison which Folsom men hunted.*

Plate 2. A Folsom point. Lindenmeier site, Colorado.

Plate 3. A flint point in place (at tip of trowel) in Sandia Cave, near Albuquerque, New Mexico.

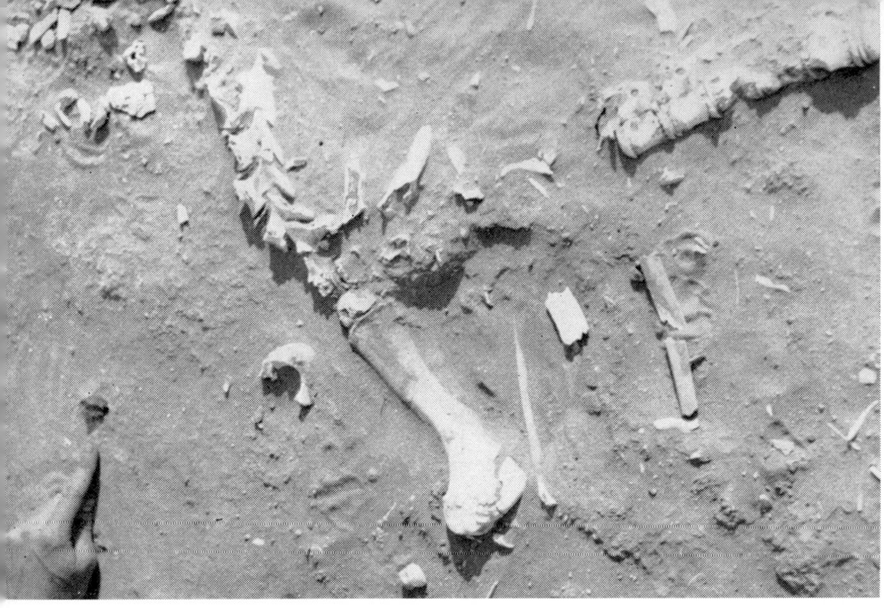

Plate 4. Point in the body of a dire wolf. Blackwater Draw, New Mexico.

Plate 5. Archaeologists excavating bones of mammoth near Dent, Colorado.

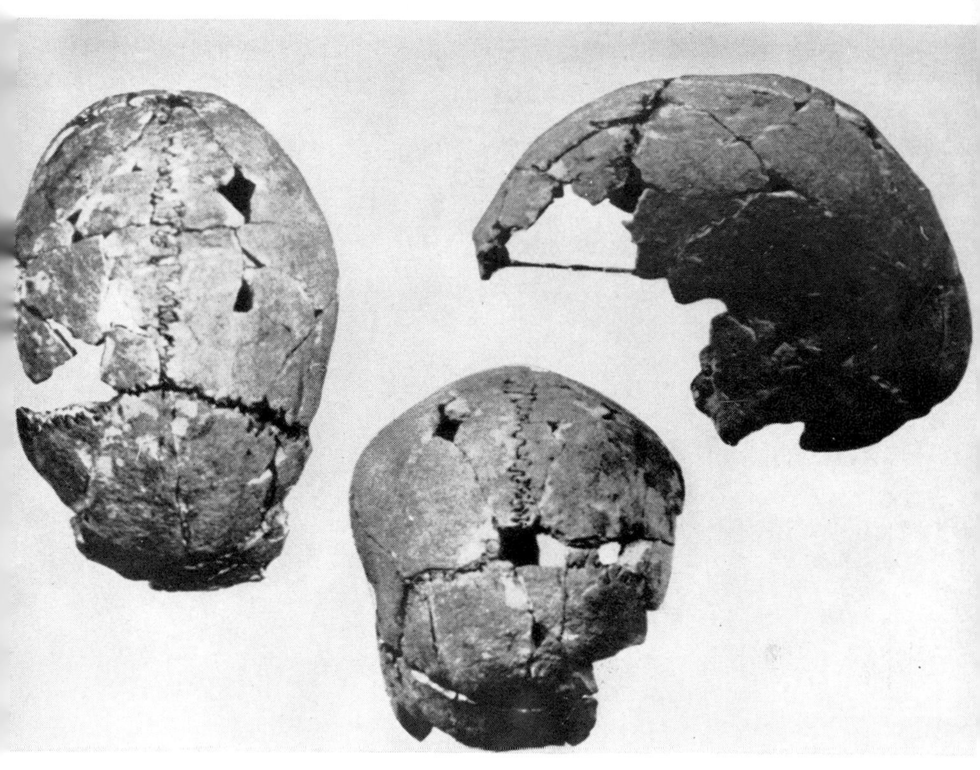

Plate 6. Skull of Midland woman. Midland, Texas.

Plate 7. Birds-eye view of Cahokia Mound. East St. Louis, Illinois.

Plate 8. Pearls perforated for stringing. From central altar of mound. Madisonville, Ohio.

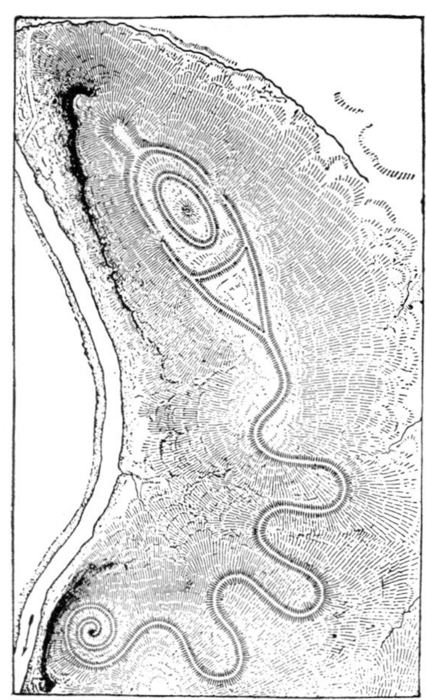

*Plate 9.
Holmes' figure of the
Serpent Mound. Ohio.*

Plate 10. Two shell gorgets, worn suspended at the neck for ornament. Specimen on the left shows a warrior holding a severed human head in one hand and a ceremonial knife or weapon in the other. Figure on right displays a common decorative motif of Etowah culture—the pileated woodpecker. From the Etowah Group, Georgia.

Plate 11. Sculptured sacred image. From the Etowah Group, Cartersville, Georgia.

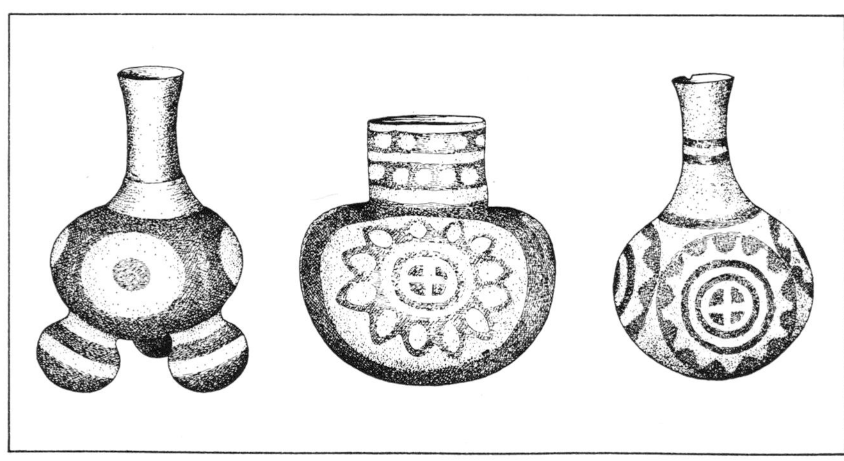

Plate 12. Pottery water bottles from graves. From Temple Mound, Etowah site, Georgia.

Plate 13. Closely woven basket, one foot, five and one-half inches in diameter. Found in cave, Grand Gulch, Utah.

late 14.
'rehistoric bag made of
ucca fiber.
'rom cliff ruins,
;rand Gulch, Utah.

Plate 15. Mesa Verde, Colorado.

Plate 16. The White House. Prehistoric cliff dwellings. Canyon de Chelley, Arizona.

Plate 17. Rich diggings. A number of Pueblo burials, each with bowls of food, in a trash mound below a ruin near Jemez, New Mexico.

*Plate 18.
A Pueblo burial. Bowls of food were placed with the dead. Pueblo of Kuaua (now called Coronado's Monument).*

Plate 19. Excavations on buildings I and II. Pueblo San Cristobal, New Mexico.

*Plate 20.
Excavation of
small pueblo of
Pueblo II period.
Kiva in foreground.
Chaco Canyon,
New Mexico.*

Plate 21. Pottery from Chaco Canyon, New Mexico.

Plate 22. Chaco black on white pottery. (Pottery pipe in center.) From Chaco Canyon, New Mexico.

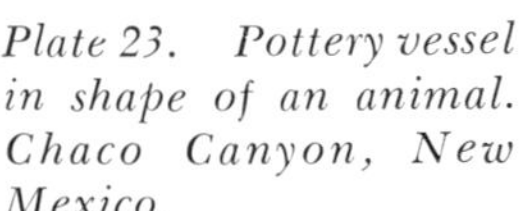

Plate 23. Pottery vessel in shape of an animal. Chaco Canyon, New Mexico.

Plate 24. Pueblo Bonito. Chaco Canyon, New Mexico.

Plate 25. Pottery. Pueblo Bonito, New Mexico.

Plate 26. Stone lamp. Amaknak, Aleutian Islands.

Plate 27. Muck deposits of Alaska. Wood and bones frozen in the mixed mass. Near Cripple Creek, Alaska.

Plate 28. Ivory seal from the buried city of Ipiutak, northwest Alaska.

8

Mound Mystery Solved

EVEN Squier and Davis in their survey of the mound area did not discover who the Mound Builders were. They made a number of romantic speculations in their book, *Ancient Monuments of the Mississippi Valley,* but these speculations asked more questions than they answered. It was obvious that the riddle of the mounds was not going to be solved by accurate surveys and geographical descriptions.

Out of an era of speculation and romance and indiscriminate collecting came William Mills of the Ohio State Museum. Dr. Mills himself had been a collector in his early years, but he had found that accumulating relics did not solve the mystery.

So, in 1900, William Mills began to dig. He made a point of digging in places which were not of themselves spectacular. He excavated not only the ceremonial earthworks described by Squier and Davis, but he also grubbed in the sites of the villages in which mound-building people had lived. He combed their garbage piles and examined their broken and discarded trash. It was from such often unspectacular bits that archaeologist Mills derived his greatest information.

Encouraged by the digging in Ohio in the early 1900s, other archaeologists in other states began to excavate. Dr. Fay-Cooper Cole began to dig in the state of Illinois. Another archaeologist, Warren Moorehead, excavated in Georgia. A Kentucky archaeologist, W. S. Webb, began to dig in the Blue Grass State. Through the 1920s and into the 1930s, more and more careful digging was done. In many cases the excavators had to go back to the tumbled spoil piles which careless collectors had already dug up. They found in places that the precious information they sought had been destroyed. But they were able to begin, methodically and slowly, to reconstruct the story of the mounds and their builders from the fragments they did find.

Archaeologists were soon able to recognize kinds of mounds, and variations of Mound Builder artifacts to which they gave specific names. Scientists learned too that not all the Mound Builders had lived at the same time. There had not been a single golden era during which these people had piled up great monuments of earth. In Ohio, for example, Dr. Mills found the great geometric earthwork of a people he identified as "Hopewell" Mound Builders. The name had originated when mounds of that kind had first been scientifically excavated on the farm of Mrs. Hopewell near Chillicothe, Ohio. In the layer above the Hopewell relics, Mills and his archaeological crew had found remains of another tribe of Mound Builders called Fort Ancient. Since the Fort Ancient layer was above the Hopewell, it would seem that the Fort Ancient people were later than the Hopewell people.

But at the time of Dr. Mills' death in 1928, the major questions about mound-building people remained unanswered. An assistant of Dr. Mills, H. C. Shetrone, carried on the good work. Shetrone asked archaeologists from all over the United States to come to Ohio to help solve the problem. Other archaeologists dug in every state east of the Mississippi and in several west of the river. By their combined efforts, they solved the mystery.

In general, there were two major kinds of mound structures. In the northern Mississippi and throughout New England, most of the mounds are round or conical affairs. These simple "tumuli" are usually of modest size, seldom over 20 or 30 feet high. Those who excavated them invariably found skeletons inside. For this reason, the tumulus mounds are usually called "burial mounds." The mound Thomas Jefferson dug on his farm in Virginia was of this kind.

In the southern Mississippi Valley, extending from St. Louis southward to the Gulf Coast, most of the mounds are flat-topped and square or rectangular. Most of them are two or more levels high and have a truncated shape. Very seldom have flat-topped mounds been found to contain burials. We now know that most of these mounds were not built for funeral purposes but as foundations for wooden buildings or temples. They are thus called temple or flat-topped mounds.

In addition to these two major types of mounds, archaeologists began to identify many others. Another variety, found in the Ohio Valley and extending through Indiana, Illinois, and west to Iowa, is the geometric work which so intrigued Squier and Davis. These works consist of earthen embankments 15 or 20 feet high which are formed into circles, squares, octagons, parallel-walled "passways," and semicircular forms. The geometric works often enclosed, in an earthen-walled circle or square, an area of a hundred of more acres. Often, also, they had tumuli or burial mounds placed symmetrically throughout their plan.

Another class of Mound Builder edifices is the fortified hill. Some of these are found in every state east of the Mississippi, and a concentration of such military fortresses exists in Ohio, Kentucky, and Tennessee. Probably not all of them were built by the same tribe of Mound Builders, as they show many variations in manufacture and plan. They all consist of earth or stone or both, piled on top of an isolated hill for an enclosed fortification. Accessible portions of the hill were usually fortified with a single or double row of earthen walls with strategically placed gateways and sally ports. Steeper areas and less accessible approaches were fortified by lower walls. Probably most of these earth embankments were topped by wooden palisades to make the fortification stronger. Some of the hilltop forts enclosed as much as 200 acres and were fitted with artificial reservoirs to supply water during a siege.

Quite another type of mound is the effigy mound, built in the shape of a bird, animal, snake, or man. The effigy mounds are usually of moderate height with rounded contours. They occur mostly in groups. The effigies in many cases suggest by their outline not only a bird but a species of bird such as an eagle or a swallow. Bears, turtles, foxes, and other animals were faithfully outlined by Mound Builder artists. Human burials were placed at such points in the effigy as the head or the heart. The effigy mounds may be considered a fancy variation of the ordinary burial mound. Quite often, round burial tumuli were built with a group of effigy mounds. Effigy mounds are heavily concentrated in the region of Wisconsin, although they are found scattered elsewhere. The famous Serpent Mound in Ohio is of this type. The Opossum Mound in Tennessee is an effigy mound which may or may not have been built by the same ancient architects as the Wisconsin effigies.

There are a number of variations in addition to these kinds of Mound Builder edifices. Archaeologists found that in certain parts of Ohio, Kentucky, and West Virginia they were able to identify a "chocolate drop" mound. This is a tumulus with a round base and a pointed conical shape. Some of them are very large and high and very symmetrical in outline. One such, the Miamisburg Mound at Miamisburg, Ohio, is 78 feet high. The famous Grave Creek Mound near Wheeling, West Virginia, also has the pointed conical shape.

In Missouri, archaeologists identified "garden mounds." In east Texas, "ring mounds" seemed indicative of a different kind of ancient activity. In the swampy regions of the Florida Keys, artificial plazas, lagoons, platforms, and canals mark the activity of Mound Builder peoples there.

The various types of mounds were consistently associated with different kinds of pottery, copper, bone, and shell. Through the latter, scientists could identify the different kinds of people. They gave these ancient tribes names, usually from the place where they were first found, for in every case the original name had been lost. Thus Georgia archaeologists began to speak of the Etowah people, named from the mound group on the Etowah River. In Alabama it was the Moundville tribe which had built the great flat-topped mounds at Moundville on the Black Warrior River. In Tennessee it was the Candy Creek people, and so on. In every place that the Mound Builders had left their earthen monuments, archaeologists gave them names. Various groups of early mound-building people who built the same kinds of mounds were obviously related and had the same general religious customs. Varieties of pottery as well as kinds of stone, shell, and metal work found in or around mounds were further clues as to relationships of tribes, trade connections, and political alliances.

One of the greatest difficulties was that a number of ancient people in the eastern part of North America did not build mounds either of the round burial variety or the flat-topped kind. Archaeologists suspected that these non-mound-building people were earlier than the rest. But there was no definite proof.

However, there were questions which had not been answered. Where had these people come from and where had they gone? How old were most of the mounds? Where had the idea of building mounds come from in the first place?

Drawing upon experience in other areas, a number of archaeologists in the mound area tried to use dendrochronology, or tree-ring time. Dr. Florence Ellis, one of the original students of Dr. Douglass of Arizona, came to the Mississippi Valley in 1937 to work out a master chart for tree-ring dating. Dr. Ellis worked for over four years in the middle Mississippi area. The results were very disappointing indeed.

Very little wood has been found in the mounds, for the damp clays of the humid valleys in which the mounds are located are not conducive to its preservation. But despite adverse conditions, occasionally enough of a charred beam or fire-blackened post was preserved for the dendrochronologist to get a cross-section and examine the telltale rings. Charcoal usually preserves very well. Dr. Ellis managed to salvage a few dozen specimens from some selected mounds in the area.

But tree-ring time did not work well in the Mississippi. Dr. Ellis found most of the trees in the river valleys to be "complacent." This means that their rings were so even in growth that they did not form a significant chart. The wet and dry periods of the Mississippi Valley of long ago were not definite or long enough to produce the wide and narrow rings which enable scientists to set dates. Dr. Ellis made some educated guesses as to when certain mounds were built, but she could not be sure.

Where one scientific method failed, another one was successful. With the development of radioactive dating by carbon 14, mound after mound yielded the secret of its time. Some of the results were astounding. Dating for the most part from pieces of charcoal found in the mounds, laboratory technicians counted very carefully the radioactive pulses that emanated from these long-dead embers. The dates ranged all the way from an astounding 10,000 years ago for some pre-mound-building people in the Modoc Cave in Illinois to recent dates of 1,000 A.D. or later for Mound Builders in the southern Mississippi Valley. As more and more carbon 14 dates were determined by archaeologists, the whole chronological picture became clear. In some ways, the old romanticists had been right. Certain pre-mound-building people had lived in the valleys of eastern North America thousands of years ago. Less romantic writers had been right also, in that some of the mounds were built very recently indeed. Historian archaeologists soon demonstrated that at least a few Mound Builders were still building mounds in historical times. Spanish explorers of the sixteenth century such as Cabeza de Vaca, Hernando de Soto, and Tristan de Luna, who penetrated the southeastern part of the United States, had actually seen Indians still building earthen mounds. The early romanticists had missed this evidence entirely.

It was still not known how the practice of mound-building had entered the New World. Long before this art had been introduced some 6,000 to 8,000 years ago, people had lived in the valleys of the Ohio, the Tennessee, the Savannah, and in other favorable spots in eastern North America. These early people lived by food gathering and hunting. Archaeologists call these pre-mound-building people *Archaic.*

Archaic people built the great fish weir found beneath Boston. In Kentucky, archaic tribesmen gathered and ate fresh-water clams and piled their shells in heaps scattered along the banks of the rivers. In Georgia, archaic food gatherers lived in the valleys and hunted small game and gathered fruit and nuts and wild berries. In most cases the archaic people did not have pottery. They did not build elaborate homes and at first they did not build mounds.

Then the art of mound-building was introduced about 1000 B.C. Almost certainly the building of mounds was introduced into the Mississippi Valley from some area where the practice had been going on for a very long time. The earliest kinds of mounds are the rounded burial mounds. These seemed to be the most prolific in the Upper Mississippi Valley. Some of the very earliest burial mounds, by carbon 14, showing dates of 700 B.C. are in Ohio, Indiana, and Illinois. Where could the idea have come from? The first mound-building seems to have begun in the very middle of the North American continent.

Some archaeologists suggested that the art of mound-building had been introduced from Mexico. In Mexico and Central America the Indians had developed earthen pyramids, in some cases building them of stone. But no trail of earthen mounds could be traced from the Valley of Mexico northward to the Mississippi. In any case, the Mexicans had never made rounded burial mounds of earth.

Perhaps, argued other scientists, the art of mound-building came across the Bering Strait from Asia. Mounds and mound-building were common in Asia in early times. The Russian steppes are dotted with burial mounds dating from Neolithic times through the Bronze Age and later. But, argued others, there are no mounds in Alaska or in northern Canada. How could Mound Builders have moved from ancient Siberia to the Upper Mississippi Valley and left no mounds along their trail?

Pottery also appeared with the early burial mounds. Most of these early pottery vessels were decorated with the imprints of twisted cords. The ancient potters had produced this effect by wrapping a piece of string around a wooden paddle and patting the outside of the clay vessels with them while the clay was still plastic. Cord-marked pottery also is found in central Siberia and extends into European Russia. There seemed to be no intrinsic meaning to this design, and it seems possible that it came into America from Asia.

If cord-marked pottery came that way, why not mounds? And so the controversy goes on. Some archaeologists are indignant at the idea of deriving mounds and mound-building from Asia, and insist that the practice was originated and developed by the Americans themselves.

Wherever mound-building originated, it began in this country in the Upper Mississippi Valley about 1000 B.C. With mound-building appeared agriculture and the making of pottery. Curiously enough, some of the earliest mounds were the most elaborate. Some of the very first mound-building groups were the most highly organized and their religious rituals were the most colorful. The Hopewell people, who built the elaborate earthworks of the Ohio Valley, belonged to this first period. So did the builders of the effigy mounds of Wisconsin. It was in the very early days of mound-building that the farthest trade connections were established.

Scientific excavations in the burial mounds of this brilliant epoch of American prehistory revealed the existence of ancient kings and princes. Some of these were found when H. C. Shetrone of the Ohio State Museum dug the Seip Mound near Chillicothe, Ohio, in 1927. The Seip Mound, named from the Seip brothers who owned the land, was a large burial mound, part of a geometric enclosure built by the Hopewell people. It contained ninety-nine burials. Many of the people buried here had been cremated. All had obviously been people of importance. The burials were lavishly accompanied by copper breastplates, copper headdresses and ear spools, mica mirrors, shell drinking cups, and other paraphernalia which only an important prince of the Hopewell people might have possessed. One of the burials contained four persons. The skeletons were not cremated as most of the others had been, but lay side by side. Apparently the four had died at the same time. Over the four bodies the priests had placed as an offering some twenty gallons of fresh-water pearls. By modern standards, this cache of gems might be worth two million dollars or more. They are still beautiful after having been buried for centuries in the moist earth. Who were these four people who commanded such wealth and respect? The Seip Mound is surrounded by a great circular embankment and also a square typical of Hopewell ceremonial buildings. Perhaps one of the skeletons was that of the architect of this mortuary temple, or perhaps a king who had been buried with the pearls as a tribute from his subjects.

As each of the burial mounds was excavated by archaeologists, fragments of early American history began to emerge. Just as in ancient Egypt, where the pharaohs and members of the royal house commanded enough wealth and manpower to build their tombs, so also did the rulers of the American Mound Builders. Unfortunately, the people of burial mound times never evolved a written language. We have no inscriptions which give the names of the princes and chieftains and tell of their deeds.

By carbon 14 dating, and by other archaeological means, it was soon determined that the flat-topped or temple mounds came later than the burial mounds. The flat-topped or pyramid mounds were built in the centuries following the birth of Christ, and most of them dated around 1000 A.D. The flat-topped mounds also were distributed in the middle Mississippi and the southern reaches of the Mississippi system.

Although there is uncertainty about the origin of the burial mounds, the origin of the flat-topped pyramid mounds has been traced. Some of these mounds were built with slanted ramps or stairways leading to their summits. Many were built in terraces of diminishing size rising to a truncated summit. Most of the flat-topped mounds were surmounted by a wooden structure or temple. Both in use and in appearance the temple mounds of the southern Mississippi are similar to the terraced pyramids and flat-topped mounds which were built in early times in Mexico. There are mounds of this kind in northern Mexico, but again there is an inexplicable gap in the mound-building evidence between northern Mexico and eastern Texas where the mounds begin again. Perhaps, suggest some archaeologists, the art of building temple mounds was brought by ancient Mexicans traveling by canoe along the Gulf Coast. Certainly agriculture moved into the Mississippi Valley from Mexico and Central America. The art of pottery making probably also came from a southern source. Why not temple mounds and the ceremonialism which went with them?

The Mexican origin of the temple mounds has been established by the discovery of articles with the flat-topped mounds of the southern region of North America which are clearly derived from Mexican culture. Around the temple mounds are cemeteries where the Temple Mound Builders buried their dead. In these cemeteries, and also in ceremonial caches nearby, many evidences of the art and handiwork of the Temple Mound Builders have been found. Like the burial mound people farther north, these people worked in copper and shell and stone. But their art work is very different from that of the Hopewell people of Ohio, for example. The Temple Mound Builders carved copper plaques and shell neck pieces with typical intricate linear designs. These designs show dancing priests with elaborate feather headdresses. The swastika is a common motif. Characteristic also are eagles, herons, woodpeckers, and other birds, all in linear carvings arranged in symmetrical and elaborate designs. A group of motifs typical of the Temple Mound Builders seems to be an indication of ceremonies which had to do with death. They carved on shell, stone, copper, and pottery motifs such as severed human hands, human skulls, severed human arms with the bones protruding, and human hearts. We know that the Mexicans practiced human sacrifice atop their pyramids. There is good evidence that the Temple Mound Builders did also. The severed hands, fingers, arms, and heads which appear in their designs are probable indications of a "death cult."

In a few places in the southeastern United States, Temple Mound Builders were still at work when the first Spanish explorers landed on the coast. But the era of the temple mounds was already past when de Soto and De Luna made their exploratory trips into the Southeast in the sixteenth century. Most of the temples had already rotted and collapsed by the time European settlers had moved into these areas. The grisly rites which had been enacted in these temples were forgotten and the people with them.

By digging, archaeologists have been able to rescue much of this history from oblivion. The archaeologist Warren Moorehead excavated the group of flat-topped mounds at Etowah, Georgia, in 1925. Here he found evidence of a flourishing and highly organized tribe of Temple Mound Builders. They had built a gigantic flat-topped mound 66 feet high and covering three acres of ground. On top of this pyramid of earth and also on the summits of other flat-topped pyramids of the Etowah group, they had built wooden structures in honor of their gods. In the graves surrounding the mounds Moorehead found *repoussé* copper plates with designs of human figures and birds, engraved shells, and intricately carved and chipped stone objects. The art of the Etowah people showed that they too had some kind of death cult. Their techniques rivaled in splendor those of the Hopewell burial mound artists. Certainly the Etowah chieftains were as important and their history as significant.

And yet when Garsilaso de la Vega, the chronicler of de Soto's expedition, recorded in 1723 the passage of the Spanish explorers along the Etowah River, the Temple Mound Builders of Etowah had already disappeared and their wooden temples rotted away. Only the great earthen mounds, the foundations of these temples, remained to mark where a great people had been.

Another center of the Temple Mound Builders is at Moundville, Alabama. Here ancient artisans had built 19 flat-topped mounds in a great group. Here also they had left evidence of their high artistic skill. Their artistry contained the macabre motifs of the death cult. At Moundville, as in the other places, archaeologists have, by painstaking effort, wrested pieces of ancient history from the clues which the Temple Mound Builders left behind.

The builders of flat-topped mounds penetrated as far up the Mississippi Valley as southern Wisconsin. In many cases they conquered the earlier burial mound peoples.

The largest mound of any type is a flat-topped mound in East St. Louis. This is the Cahokia Mound or, as it is sometimes called, the "Monks' Mound" because at one time a group of Trappist monks built a monastery on its summit. The Monks' Mound is a great pyramid which rises by four stages to reach a height of just over 100 feet. The base of the great mound covers 16 acres. Originally, Monks' Mound dominated a group of more than 100 flat-topped mounds arranged in the surrounding river bottom. Within seven miles of the Monks' Mound are additional mound groups comprising more than 300 flat-topped mounds in all. The Cahokia concentration of temple mounds is as impressive as many of the clusters of pyramids in the Valley of Mexico itself. The population of Temple Mound Builders at Cahokia was probably as great in its heyday as the present population of St. Louis and the surrounding towns.

With the excavations of archaeologists in these many places where the Mound Builders had lived and died, fragments of early American history were pulled from the earth and put together into a pattern. The major questions of the mystery of the mounds were answered. Early archaic people, perhaps 10,000 years ago, had started life in what is now the eastern United States. The secret of agriculture to these archaic people had come from the south where it began. In the centuries before the birth of Christ, kings and princes arose among them. They developed an integrated society and established trade connections, and about 1000 B.C. they began to build great mounds and earthworks to the glory of their dead.

The burial mound epoch was followed by the temple mound period which extended almost to historic times. The Temple Mound Builders almost certainly derived their inspiration from Mexico. Perhaps the first temple mounds were actually built in the southern Mississippi Valley by Mexican emissaries. But by the time the Mexican empire in the Valley of Mexico had risen to an apex under the great Montezuma in the sixteenth century, the flat-topped mounds of the Mississippi Valley had already fallen into disuse. The temple mound era, its people dead and its ceremonies forgotten, passed into oblivion. Most of the modern Indian tribes with whom the Europeans came into contact no longer built mounds or practised the ceremonies which went with them.

Why did the custom of mound-building pass? Why did the highly organized Mound Builder societies dissolve and disappear? High civilizations have risen and fallen before and undoubtedly will again. Rude and barbaric people have overthrown highly organized societies previously in history. With further digging in the mounds, we will find the answers to some of the questions. With every fragment of information a part of the picture becomes clearer. Each lesson from the past is a help for the future.

9

Dams and Diggers

A HUGE TRACTOR with caterpillar treads moved along the river bank dragging behind it a scoop shovel as big as a moving van. As the edge bit into the soft earth, it crushed through fragments of pottery and bone tools. In the wide furrow in the wake of this mechanical monster was a streak of charcoal scraped from an ancient fireplace. There were the stumps of posts which had once formed walls. A human skeleton laid bare by the moving scraper was partially rolled from the grave where it had lain for hundreds of years.

An archaeologist darted forward to retrieve the skeleton. He motioned authoritatively to the operator of the tractor to direct the equipment to scrape up earth in some other spot. The archaeologist called two assistants and they knelt to examine the posts and the fire pit. These were the remains of a squarish house. The pottery and tools scattered on the hard earth floor had been left by people who had once lived there.

Certainly no archaeologist in his right mind would ever use an earth-moving monster for modern excavation. And yet this archaeologist was doing just that. The whole trend of modern archaeological technique has been toward more careful methods rather than the contrary. Earlier despoilers of ancient sites might have used mechanical scrapers for "potato digs," but certainly no contemporary scientist would employ such destructive and rapacious methods. The modern archaeologist is trained to employ the trowel and the whisk broom with a skillfully delicate touch and to use dental tools for really fine work.

When Elephant Butte Dam was first constructed in the Rio Grande Valley in 1915, the imprisoned waters soon flooded some twelve ancient Indian pueblos and an unknown number of other sites and caves of earlier people. Soon the sediment carried into the reservoir by the muddy Rio Grande buried these ancient places in tens of feet of muddy ooze. Even if Elephant Butte Lake should be drained, the eyes of man will never again look upon those archaeological treasures. A few antiquarians who noticed that the Elephant Butte project had destroyed a goodly amount of the archaeological record of the area remarked at the time that it was too bad, but nobody did anything about it.

During the 1930s, a dozen more dams were built at various places in the United States. Each of these backed up reservoirs which covered ancient sites. At the same time the first great pipelines for carrying natural gas and oil were laid across sections of the United States. The pipeline layers developed clever mechanical diggers. These machines crawled across the countryside whirling iron buckets which scooped out a deep trench in which the pipes were to be laid. As the ditch diggers dug, they sliced through many ancient places. Occasionally the pipeline workers were able to salvage an odd skull, a carved bit of stone, or a pottery vessel. There were stories of pipeline cuts that had gone through whole ancient towns, mounds, burned houses, and cemeteries full of skeletons. But few of these were saved and none noted scientifically. By comparison, during these years archaeologists were digging puny holes in various places in which they hoped to find the story of American antiquity. The pipeline diggers, road crews, and dam builders were digging or covering up areas many thousands of times larger than those which the archaeologists were able to examine.

After the Second World War, new and greater projects were contemplated. The Congress of the United States, in its wisdom, passed bills providing for the erection of a whole series of dams in the Missouri Valley and its tributaries. These mighty projects would require the moving of millions of cubic yards of earth and the inundation of square miles of river bottom when the dams were finished. Archaeologists, especially those at the National Museum in Washington, were appalled at the impending loss to archaeology in these important areas. They managed to persuade Congress that the American people *were* interested in their own antiquity, and so funds for the archaeological examination of the areas to be affected were added to the original congressional appropriations. The most important area and the major problem lay in the Missouri Valley. The ensuing archaeological dig became known as the River Basin Survey. It is undoubtedly the largest archaeological excavation ever undertaken.

In other places, in New Mexico, Colorado, Utah, Idaho, Oregon, Arizona, and California, dams and public works projects included in their planning the salvage of archaeological sites which would otherwise have been destroyed. State highway departments, notoriously practical in all matters pertaining to finances, enlisted crews of archaeologists to salvage archaeological material which was revealed when new roads were laid out or old highways widened or straightened. Even close-fisted gas companies and oil firms, when they laid out a new pipeline route, sent a crew of archaeologists ahead of the ditch-digging machines to salvage archaeological information. Then the archaeologists followed up by examining the walls of newly cut trenches to see if they contained any evidence of antiquity. A great number of recent books and publications have resulted from these activities. Some of the archaeological salvage operations, by necessity, were done hastily. However, had they not been carried out in connection with the commercial programs, most of them would not have been done at all. One great difficulty has been acquiring enough trained archaeologists to direct all the digging activities. Hundreds of competent diggers were needed. Undoubtedly many times this number will be required in the future as such salvage programs multiply.

The most revealing discoveries to come out of the welter of digging activity were made in the Great Plains in central North America. The Plains area had been largely neglected by archaeologists—for good reason. For one thing, there is little surface evidence in the Plains that any great civilizations ever existed there. There are no pyramid temples, or great stone pueblos, or even earthen mounds. The Mound Builders extended into the eastern periphery of the Plains, and there their activity ceased. In the high prairies, scientists had found little evidence of ancient life on the surface. When the "sod busters" followed the plainsmen into the prairies and overturned the rich soil with their mold-board plows, they uncovered some pieces of crudely made pottery, arrowheads, and beds of charcoal, but there was little concrete evidence of architecture and certainly no indications of a high civilization. Most archaeologists passed over the prairies as being unimportant to archaeology.

It was not until 1933 that any serious effort was made to discover what the ancient life of the Great Plains had been. By this time it was known that Sandia and Folsom men had hunted Ice Age animals there thousands of years ago. But nothing noteworthy was discovered about the times which followed. Dr. William Duncan Strong decided to make an archaeological survey of the state of Nebraska. Strong felt that, as Nebraska was the heart of the Great Plains, the archaeological remains he might discover there would provide the solution to the problem. They did.

Dr. Strong found out what many modern Nebraskan farmers already knew. Along the river bottoms and stream banks were many evidences of the villages and towns of ancient people. These people had made pottery. They had made earthen lodges which were dug partly into the surface of the ground, and they had undoubtedly practiced agriculture. In places, the plows of present-day farmers had ripped into storage pits dug into the hard earth. In these storage pits were charred corn cobs left there by ancient agriculturists.

Dr. Strong found that some ancient farmers had been in the Great Plains for a very long time. There were crude farming villages which seemed to go back hundreds and perhaps thousands of years. Beginning crudely, the agricultural way of life had reached a flourishing climax. Hundreds of towns had lined the rivers of the Great Plains. The farmers of long ago had planted corn and beans and squash in the same soil now tilled by prosperous modern farmers of Nebraska and the other Plains states. By studying their pottery, the kinds of houses they lived in, and the tools they made, Dr. Strong was able to distinguish two major kinds of early Plains farmers. He called one of these the "Nebraskan people," and the other the "Upper Republicans" because he found so many of their towns along the course of the Upper Republican River.

When the archaeologists of the River Basin Survey began to examine the valley areas which were to be flooded by new dams, they discovered ancient agricultural villages everywhere. Hundreds of farming towns of long ago were situated along the river terraces, especially along the Missouri and its many tributaries. So numerous were the towns that the archaeologists could not excavate them all. In many places they were able only to sample the towns by digging two or three houses out of the total number. In other spots, the mechanical scoops of the dam builders themselves revealed other villages and towns of the farming people as they cleared earth for sluiceways and coffer dams. During these activities, the diggers also found evidences of early Ice Age hunters. Occasionally they discovered the deeply buried fire hearths of the food gathering people who lived at the end of the Ice Age. And scattered everywhere were the tepee rings of the buffalo-hunting Indians of modern times. But mostly the dam diggers found the village cultures of the farming era.

It was obvious from the first that there were more than two kinds of ancient farmers, as Dr. Strong had thought. As the archaeologists excavated first one village and then another, they were able to distinguish a number of kinds of houses, fortifications, pottery, and tools. All the houses of the farmers had been dug down a foot or two into the surface of the soil. This undoubtedly made the homes more snug when winter blizzards swept over the prairies. The houses were covered over with a framework of poles, bark, and earth. But within this general arrangement were many variations. Some of the earthen lodges were rounded; others were square. Usually a farming village consisted of a dozen or more earthen lodge houses. In some towns, the lodges were arranged formally in a single or double row. Other villages had not been so carefully planned and the houses were placed haphazardly.

With the advent of agriculture on the Great Plains, there had also appeared warfare, which is a usual accompaniment of civilization. Some of the village towns along the Missouri were fortified. At some sites the river banks themselves formed part of the fortification and were often augmented with walls of earth surmounted by palisades. Digging in other villages revealed that no protective measures had been taken. The fortifications or lack of fortifications gave historical information about the movements and countermovements of hostile tribes.

But mostly the archaeologists concerned themsleves with pottery. Always, when an ancient people takes up the practice of agriculture, they also begin to make pottery. Pottery is impractical among hunting people, but it is very useful for preparing and storing agricultural food products. An ancient clay container is just a pot to the layman, and undoubtedly was just a bean kettle to someone who inhabited the Missouri Valley 500 years ago. But to an archaeologist this pottery vessel is a source of information. The shape of the pot, the kind of clay of which it is made, the broken-up rock or "temper" which is mixed with the clay to keep the pot from cracking—all are valuable archaeological clues. Especially revealing is the decoration of the surface of the vessel, for scarcely any of these ancient utensils were plainly made. The commonest tradition of decoration on the Great Plains of long ago was the cordmarking discussed earlier. Many village potters of the ancient Plains towns cord-marked their pottery, but they did it in different ways. Archaeologists soon discovered what these differences were.

The implements of the Plains farmers also varied from village to village. Some had squash knives made of the shoulder blades of elk. Others had hoes with which they cultivated their fields. These hoes were usually made of bone and were distinctive in shape and in the way in which the handle was attached. There were distinctive kinds of knives, of both bone and stone. Especially revealing were the tobacco pipes. The early Plains farmers, like almost all early American agriculturists, grew and used tobacco. The shape of the pipes they used were indicative of different traditions. Some were tubular. Others were elbow-shaped. The elbow pipe is typical of the Upper Republican farmers. Still other pipes were made of clay, sometimes decorated with human faces or the heads of animals such as those used by the Nebraskan people.

Every fall, after the excavating season had drawn to a close, the archaeologists brought their pottery, tools, and information to a central laboratory at the University of Nebraska at Lincoln. During the winter months, they pooled their information and worked over their material. The results were astonishing. Far from discovering a few tribes of Indians who had practiced agriculture on a marginal scale, they found village cultures of the Great Plains in which a whole complex of tribes practiced agriculture on an extensive scale. Archaeologists, after several years of excavation and investigation in the dam areas, began to speak of a Central Plains Tradition, a Middle Missouri Tradition, and the Upper Missouri Villages. Within each of these traditions they began to distinguish the farming towns of individual tribes. By careful archaeological sleuthing, they were able to follow the movements of some of these people. They found out which ones were enemies, what they considered their territory, and how they held or defended it.

Most important of all, perhaps, they were able to date the farming towns of the Plains fairly accurately. Most of these places had been occupied by agricultural peoples only a few hundred years ago. Most of the farming tribes had lived in the Great Plains and cultivated their maize fields there in the 1300s and 1400s of our era. Some of the agricultural villages had lasted almost into historical times. The agricultural idea had come from Mexico or from the American Southwest but much later than the influences which began the mound-building era to the east.

When, in the sixteenth century, the French Jesuits pushed into the area which is now the Dakotas, they found the Knife River villages of the Hidatsa Indians in what is now North Dakota. The Hidatsas were still living in earthen lodges, making pottery, and growing fields of maize around their towns. The Pawnees, a tribe of eastern Nebraska, were also still living in villages and growing agricultural products when the French traders first visited them. And there were other village farmers, especially on the eastern edges of the Great Plains, still carrying on this way of life, at the same time that European colonists were establishing themselves on the eastern coast and the European occupation of America was well on its way.

Although it might be thought that the Europeans brought an end to the farming cultures of the Great Plains, descriptions of the first explorations into the prairie area refute this idea. Early traders and scouts found the Indian tribes on the Great Plains already hunting buffalo and practicing warfare. What had happened?

In other places in ancient America, agriculture had led to true civilization. The Mound Builders, with a way of life based on agriculture, had developed a complex ceremonial culture. They had learned to work stone and metal. They also had traded for obsidian, mica, shells, and copper over widespread areas of North America. Why did not the farmers of the Great Plains towns also develop a great civilization?

We can only say that they didn't have time to do so. Given another few centuries, the Plains people would probably have produced a great civilization as did all the other agricultural peoples. We can only guess that these prairie farmers might eventually have begun to build stone pyramids to their gods. Perhaps, also, they would have evolved a system of writing and of keeping calendrical records, but they did not. It is true that agriculture apparently started later in the Great Plains than in the Mound Builder area or in the Southwest. But it was not this late start which defeated ultimate greatness.

A clue to the disappearance of the village farmers of the Great Plains is found in the account of the expedition of Hernando de Soto, who made a trip into the southeastern portion of what is now the United States almost simultaneously with the Coronado expedition into the American Southwest. In 1540, the de Soto group traveled from Tampa Bay in Florida northward to western North Carolina and thence west beyond the Mississippi River. West of the Mississippi on the periphery of the Great Plains, the Indians told de Soto that toward the north the country was very thinly populated, that cattle were in such plenty no maize field could be protected from them, and that the inhabitants lived on meat. The "cattle" which the Indians spoke of were undoubtedly buffalo or American bison.

Castañeda, who wrote the account of the Coronado expedition, was a member of Coronado's group when he made the famous trip up the Rio Grande Valley and thence northeastward into the western edge of the Great Plains. Castañeda also tells of some Indian towns there with gardens around them, and also mentions that "wild cows" were very numerous.

These eyewitnesses of Indian life on the Great Plains in the middle of the sixteenth century revealed two important facts. One was that some of the farming towns were still occupied at this late date. The other was that North American bison were becoming numerous.

At the end of the Ice Age, the large-bodied straight-horned bison, which the Sandia and Folsom hunters killed for food, became extinct. Replacing them in the post-glacial period was a somewhat smaller variety which we now call "Bison bison." When Europeans first viewed this animal, they mistakenly called it a "buffalo." There is no true buffalo native to North America.

Undoubtedly the North American bison was present from early recent times. There is evidence that several sub-varieties had already developed. One kind of bison had penetrated into the woodlands east of the Mississippi where it was found in small numbers even into the Colonial Period. But no variety of American bison was numerous in the very early centuries of the Christian era. Perhaps the grasslands of the great prairies had not yet developed fully. Whatever the reasons, the bison were scattered and few in number during these early centuries. The early Plains farmers were also hunters of sorts. Piles of bones left from their hunting expeditions show that they killed elk, deer, and some bison. If the bison had been present in great numbers, agriculture would have been virtually impossible. The Indians had no type of fencing to protect their fields, and herds of migrating bison would have been impossible to divert in any event. It is obvious that, during the height of the farming era on the Plains, there were no great bison herds.

During the sixteenth century the Plains bison began to increase in numbers and spread over a more extensive area. Ecological conditions often produce the sudden increase in numbers of one species of life. A combination of favorable conditions can produce a population explosion of one kind of animal. It has been suggested that the rainfall and climate of the Great Plains produced conditions ideal for the increase of the tough sod-forming prairie grasses. The farming Indians found this sod difficult to break up and cultivate with the very primitive hoes and digging sticks which they had. At the same time the luxurious prairie grasses were ideal for the increase of the bison herds.

By 1700, most of the farming communities had been abandoned. The reason was probably not only that the movement of thousands of animals destroyed the maize fields, but the nearness of the herds furnished a ready supply of meat. Another reason must have been that bison hunting was exciting, whereas hoeing a corn field is dull. Within a few decades, most of the farmers abandoned their hoes and took up bows and arrows to become bison hunters. The Great Plains farmers were the only people of ancient America to abandon agriculture once they had learned its art.

The change from farming to bison hunting involved more than a change of food. As the bison herds increased, the animals moved northward to summer pastures in the spring and southward with the coming of fall. The feeding bison also moved east and west for a fresh food supply and because of storms. A farming town on the Missouri might be close to the bison hunters one month and out of touch the next. Good bison hunters must be nomads. If they are nomads, they cannot build earthen lodges.

Their women cannot make pottery, for a pot is difficult to transport. Bison hunting produced a whole new way of life. Some tribes made the change, apparently, within ten or twenty years. They abandoned their villages along the rivers and began to live in skin tepees. They moved out into the Plains and followed the bison herds wherever they went.

Agricultural gods are different from hunting gods. The maize gods were abandoned and forgotten. The gods of the rivers and the rains were no longer important. The early Plains Indians prayed instead to the Great Spirit who guided the buffalo. Their whole life was focused around this animal.

The bison herds continued to multiply through the 1700s. But even with this vast supply of meat it was inevitable that the various hunting tribes should clash with one another. Bison-hunting territories were outlined and tenaciously held. Newcomers challenged these territories. Warfare became a major aspect of Plains life. Certainly, too, a number of the Plains tribes fought for the sheer excitement of battle. With a ready supply of meat from the abundant bison, they spent their additional time and energy at war.

Whereas the early farmers had fought one another, on occasion, for a better piece of valley land on which to raise corn, the later bison hunters fought mostly for honor's sake. They evolved a series of martial decorations which the American frontiersmen called "counting coup." The word "coup" comes from the French word for blow. A coup was a blow struck at an enemy. As the system finally developed, a coup did not necessarily have to be a mortal blow. As a matter of fact, the greatest honor accrued to a Plains warrior when he hit an enemy in battle with a "coup stick." This was a painted stick which was not a true weapon. If a man could hit a fully armed enemy with a coup stick and escape to tell the tale, he showed a contempt for his adversary which brought him the greatest honor of all. Thus, with bison hunting, the Plains tribes developed a whole new set of rules and values.

The introduction of the horse about 1700 from the Spanish settlements in New Mexico accelerated the whole process of change in the Great Plains. The horse had been a common animal during the American Ice Age. At the end of the Pleistocene, the horse became extinct in both North and South America. However, wild horses continued to exist in certain parts of Asia, where they were finally domesticated. The horse appeared first in the Near East and then in Europe. When the Spanish began their conquest of the New World, they brought horses with them. The conquistadores almost always rode stallions in battle, and there were many mares in their pack trains. Both mares and stallions escaped from these early expeditions. Within a century after the first major Spanish *entrada,* wild horses were spreading into the Great Plains of North America. Most of the tribes living there had never seen a Spaniard and had had little or no contact with other Europeans, but they began to catch and use horses. They rode the animals and they used them to carry meat and camp gear. By 1700, many Plains tribes possessed hundreds of horses and through them had increased their mobility. They could move farther and kill more bison. They could pack more meat back to their camping places. Horses also increased the area over which the Indians could wage war. The stealing of horses became a part of the complicated business of aggrandizement by military means.

When the American settlers came into the Great Plains in the nineteenth century, most of these changes had already taken place. Only a few of the village farming cultures remained. The bison-hunting way of life was in full swing. Even if the hunting tribes of the Plains had carried on their way of life for several more centuries, it is doubtful that the bison hunters would have produced a great culture. No great human accomplishments are based upon hunting and certainly none upon a career of warfare. No hunting culture has ever achieved a true civilization. The Plains way of life was colorful but certainly not outstanding in material results. Archaeologically, it has left scarcely a trace.

The end of this way of life on the Plains came with the end of the bison. It was the increase of the bison that obliterated the farming villages. It was the demise of the bison which wrote finis to the hunting era. In a few short decades the American hide hunters and the repeating rifle destroyed the great herds of bison that were the result of thousands of years of development. The bloody wars which the Plains Indians fought with the American settlers and the American army were largely caused by the destruction of the Indians' food supply. The colorful war practices of the Plains Indian added romantic overtones to his struggle for existence. When the bison were gone, the way of life which depended upon the animals disappeared quickly.

Much of this story would never have been learned if archaeologists had not dug the areas threatened by dams. The colorful life of the Plains farmers is now known in its major outlines. As archaeologists continue to dig villages before they are flooded by dams, we will come to know even more about the farming era. The development of the village agriculturists of the Great Plains was stopped in mid-course by changing events. The coming of the bison ended their civilization before it really started.

Now the descendants of the bison hunters are sedentary once again. On reservations throughout the Plains area, modern Indians are turning once again to agriculture. Many of them have blended with the American population to become engineers, teachers, and builders. After the interruption of the exciting bison-hunting years, these early Americans may yet build a great civilization on the Plains.

10

The Ancient Southwest

RICHARD WETHERILL noticed the withered human hand protruding from the crack in the rock when he first walked past the mouth of the cave. It was a wild place. The sandstone walls of the canyon which towered on both sides might have prevented human beings from ever reaching this remote spot. But the pictograph of a mountain sheep pecked into the stained rock wall showed that human beings had once actually lived in this difficult place. If there was any doubt, the dried human hand itself protruding from the crevice was evidence enough.

Richard Wetherill walked into the cave in the canyon wall. There were more pictographs and the painted outlines of human hands done in red pigment. Some of the fingers of the hands were missing. Within the cave were stone slabs set on edge and forming circles in the dusty floor. Here and there in the litter was the fragment of a basket with red and black designs. There were worn-out sandals, lengths of twisted yucca rope, and wooden-shafted spears. Wetherill walked forward and pulled at the withered human hand which had first attracted his attention. A whole body tumbled out of the crevice. When the dust cleared, Wetherill saw that it was a mummy which had originally been encased in baskets decorated with the same red and black motifs.

In this way in 1899, at a place called Grand Gulch in Utah Territory, Richard Wetherill, pioneer member of a pioneer family, started southwestern archaeology. Wetherill wasn't looking for gold in Grand Gulch. He wasn't looking for new land or anything of value. Wetherill was looking for information. He wanted to know who had pecked the petroglyphic signs into the manganese-stained sandstone wall of that desert country. He was attracted by the sheer excitement of discovering an unknown people who had once lived in that wild country. He found in the caves the desiccated bodies of a forgotten tribe. Because of the beauty of their baskets, he called these ancient people "Basket Makers."

Long before Wetherill found the first Basket Maker mummy in a cave in Grand Gulch, Utah, the Spanish conquistadores had carried their standards through northern Mexico and up the Rio Grande Valley. Coronado and his successors found about seventy-five Indian towns or pueblos still occupied in 1540 and 1541. And all about them were the ruins of other pueblo towns, in some cases only recently abandoned.

It was obvious that at one time the pueblo way of life had been very widespread. Hundreds of Indian pueblos extended from the panhandle of Texas and southwestern Kansas through southern Colorado to Utah and northern Arizona in the west. The Spaniards found groups of pueblo ruins in northern Chihuahua in Old Mexico. When they first saw the tumbled walls and ruined plazas, the inhabitants of most of these towns were already gone. It was obvious even from a casual survey of the ruined towns of the American Southwest that in previous times there had been tens of thousands of Pueblo Indians. Their numbers had shrunk to a mere remnant when the Spanish arrived. The six dozen or so pueblos which still had life were obviously the remains of a very old civilization which was coming to an end. Many American archaeologists have blamed the Spanish conquistadores for blotting out the pueblo way of life. Actually, the Spanish probably saved that portion of the civilization which remained and was tottering on the verge of oblivion when they came on the scene.

Much of the history of the last days of this "living archaeology" is recorded in Spanish annals. Spanish padres and government officials recorded the various historical events of the Pueblo people during their time. The Spanish padres built churches and chapels in the pueblos which had enough occupants left to warrant the expenditure of time and effort. According to Christian custom, the Spanish church was usually built directly over the largest kiva or ceremonial room of the pueblo concerned. But there were no books in which the Pueblo had codified their rituals. They had few tangible gods or idols which the Christian priests could destroy. Nominally, the Spaniards converted the Pueblo Indians to Christianity. However, the Indians never abandoned their ancient faith. Most modern Pueblo Indians are simultaneously pagans as well as Christians, and the ancient Pueblos used the kivas even while Mass was being held at the Christian church.

Even with Christian churches at their center, many of the pueblos declined and died. During the Pueblo revolt of 1860, the Indians rose up and ousted their Spanish masters. The Spaniards re-established their authority and brought the Indians back to the pueblos from which they had fled. Nevertheless, town after town was abandoned and became a ruin like the rest. At the turn of the present century, only about twenty-five of the pueblo towns contained living inhabitants who were carrying on their ancient way of life.

Even today, in the twenty-five pueblo towns which still have living inhabitants, rain dances and harvest dances are still held. A visitor who views these ceremonies can see living archaeology. The medicine societies which perform these ceremonies, the priests, the costumes, and the rituals have all come down many centuries from antiquity. This kind of ceremonial life would have left little trace in the tumbled ruins of some deserted pueblo town. It is a wonder that we can actually behold the last manifestations of an ancient form of American culture. The painted idols still lurk behind the altars. In contrast to other conquests which the Spanish friars made in other parts of the New World, the Pueblo Indian religion proved remarkably enduring. It still is. The Spanish, perhaps, were too practical to inquire deeply into the past of the pueblo way of life. Where had the Pueblo people come from in the first place? Were there any other ancients who lived in the Southwest even before the Pueblos built their multistoried towns?

Some of these questions were actually asked by explorers who came through the Southwest in the nineteenth century. Alexander von Humboldt, German baron and friend of Goethe, described many of the ancient edifices which he saw on his travels through northern Mexico. He speculated, too, on what these monuments might mean. Another pioneer was the Swiss traveler and scholar Adolph

Bandelier, who lived and traveled in the Southwest from 1860 to 1889. Bandelier noticed that there were different kinds of ancient ruins. He was much impressed by the obvious fact that many of these forbidding desert places had supported large populations in ancient times. What was the history of these people of old?

The questions of most of these early explorers were asked but never answered. More spectacular ruins to the south in the Valley of Mexico and Central America were attracting most European scholars. The Pueblo Indians had never evolved a system of glyphic writing. Also they had not built large stone pyramids, nor anything so spectacular as the pyramid temples of Central America. If anyone had mentioned the subject in 1900, he probably would have been told that the antiquities of the American Southwest were peripheral and unimportant.

Richard Wetherill had been born in this country. He was interested in the Southwest because it was his territory. Although he had had little formal schooling, he was very much interested in antiquity. Wetherill had noticed the pueblo ruins on the tops of mesas.

When Richard Wetherill found the Basket Maker cave in Grand Gulch, Utah, he immediately realized that it was something unusual. These people, who made such beautiful baskets and lived in the caves of the sandrock country, were obviously old. The things that they made were different from those of the Pueblo people. Wetherill thought that the Basket Makers were older than the Pueblo people. He was more correct than he knew.

Richard Wetherill and his brothers also discovered a mesa in southwestern Colorado called Mesa Verde. This mesa is cut by a number of deep canyons. Along the rock walls of these deep canyons erosion forces long ago formed a number of caves and overhangs. In these caves the

Wetherills found masonry houses several stories high, towers, sacred kivas or ceremonial rooms, and artificial terraces. They called the very first of these which they found "Cliff Palace," because it was so beautifully built.

To the Wetherills, the cliff dwellers who had inhabited the canyon houses of Mesa Verde were a mysterious long-forgotten people. Not only was their origin mysterious, but their disappearance as well. Why had these cliff dwellers of centuries ago left their homes in these hidden canyons? In places, the Wetherills found pottery vessels and stone axes lying on the floors of the empty rooms as if their owners had placed them there and then left and never returned. The Wetherill brothers excavated enthusiastically in these cliff dwellings. They exhibited collections of their archaeological finds in Denver and, later on, at the Chicago Fair of 1893-94. These exhibits aroused tremendous curiosity. Even Europeans were intrigued by the mystery of the Basket Makers and Cliff Dwellers. A young Swedish scientist, Baron Nordenskiold, spent the whole season of 1891 digging with the Wetherill brothers in the cave towns of Mesa Verde. The exhibits of Cliff Dweller relics greatly roused the interest of American archaeologists.

At the turn of the century, most American scholars were already familiar with Mayan and Mexican antiquity. Some of them had begun to excavate in the mound area. But even to these scholars, the news that there were ancient civilizations in the American Southwest came as a surprise. That the rude Indians there were capable of building multistoried houses of stone and grouping these into impressive towns was news indeed.

A few scholars began to work in the Southwest in the late 1900s. Investigators from the Smithsonian Institution were attracted to inhabited pueblos, thinking that they might contain the key to the history of the earlier people. Dr. J. Walter Fewkes worked among the Hopi towns of northern Arizona and at Mesa Verde. Fewkes mapped and excavated some of the abandoned pueblos of the Hopi country and demonstrated that these abandoned towns had been occupied by former Hopi Indians.

But it was the Wetherill brothers rather than the scholars who began southwestern archaeology. The Wetherills discovered the Basket Makers of Grand Gulch and the Cliff Dwellers of Mesa Verde. Later, when they lived at Chaco Canyon, New Mexico, they found a great center of ancient life there. Richard Wetherill, pioner archaeologist, was murdered by a Navajo Indian at Chaco Canyon in 1910.

Chief among those who, after the Wetherills, became interested in southwestern archaeology was Dr. A. V. Kidder. Dr. Kidder, educated at Harvard, had first been interested in the mounds of his native Massachusetts. He was thoroughly acquainted, also, with the history of the Mayas and the Mexicans. Kidder felt that the answer to many of the problems of antiquity lay in the American Southwest and so he and his friend S. J. Guernsey traveled to that region.

Following the lead of the Wetherills just after Richard Wetherill's murder in 1910, Kidder and Guernsey excavated a number of Basket Maker caves such as those called Sunflower Cave and White Dog Cave in the Four Corners area where Utah, Arizona, Colorado, and New Mexico come together. They found evidences of ancient life there just as the Wetherills had. From the mummies, baskets, weapons, and tools they found, they were able to reconstruct the life of an ancient people. These people were hunters and had just begun to practice agriculture. In some of the later Basket Maker deposits, pottery also appeared. These Basket Makers, then, were an early people who had been on the verge of civilized development. The Wetherills had called them Basket Makers. The name was a good one. Dr. Kidder and his associates continued to use it.

But the Cliff Dwellers and the pueblo builders presented more difficult problems. Dr. Kidder chose, as the site of his major excavation, the ancient pueblo of Pecos near the modern town of the same name in New Mexico. He might have chosen any one of literally thousands of pueblos in New Mexico or Arizona for his first dig. The pueblo of Pecos was, indeed, not as large as some ruins or as impressive as others, but he chose it because it was one of those which had still been inhabited when the Spanish came. As a matter of fact, the Spanish padres had built a church at Pecos pueblo to convert the remaining Indians to Christianity. But neither the church nor the nearness of Spanish settlements prevented its final demise. In 1838, the last of the Pecos population moved out and went to join their kinsmen at the pueblo of Jemez. The building of the church at Pecos and the final exodus of the last of its population had been recorded by the Spanish. Dr. Kidder knew that he had a terminus for his chronology. By digging from a point with a known date, he would be able to fix dates for the layers beneath it.

Through the 1920s, Dr. Kidder and his crew excavated the rooms, plazas, and kivas of ancient Pecos. They found that the town had been a very old one, established about 1300 A.D. The excavators were able to distinguish many levels in which different architecture and pottery characterized different periods.

But not all of the prehistory of the American Southwest was discovered at Pecos. In 1927, Dr. Kidder called a meeting at Pecos of all of the archaeologists working in the field. Some excavators such as Dr. Nels Nelson from the American Museum had begun digging in several ancient pueblos in the Galisteo Basin near Santa Fe. Others such as Samuel Pepper and Neil Judd had begun excavations in the large stone pueblos at Chaco Canyon where the Wetherills had lived. Frank Roberts from the National Museum had begun excavations on Basket Maker sites as well as on pueblos. Dr. Kidder felt that if all these archaeologists came together, they could, by pooling their knowledge, unravel the mysteries of the ancient past.

What Kidder had not found at Pecos, some of the others had discovered elsewhere. The Pecos Conference was a declaration of independence for southwestern archaeology. The findings of this meeting showed clearly that neither the Basket Makers nor the Pueblos were country cousins of the Mexicans. The earlier idea that the pueblos had been built by the Aztecs was obviously wrong. The ancients of the Southwest had been great in their own right. They had evolved a series of civilizations which had reached a peak some time in antiquity, just as in the mound area and in ancient Mexico these civilizations were based upon agriculture. The most important characteristic of the southwestern civilizations was masonry buildings, some of adobe and some of stone. These people had not built mounds and they did not erect large flat-topped pyramids. The ancient southwesterners, at the height of their glory, constructed large apartment-house dwellings, some of which had as many as 6,000 rooms. They also had a rich and varied ceremonial life.

As a further aid to the archaeologists who were studying the ancient Southwest, the tree-ring calendar evolved by Dr. A. E. Douglass was extremely useful. The early excavators had reckoned periods by centuries and various levels of earth. With Dr. Douglass' tree-ring time, the exact year at which some of the buildings had been erected could be calculated. Sections of wooden beams pulled from cliff dwellings and pueblos could be dated by their outside ring to tell the exact year at which that log had been cut by a stone axe.

The Pecos Archaeological Conference was only the first meeting of its kind. Every year, archaeologists gathered together to pool their interests and report upon their findings. The Pecos Conference is still held annually in the American Southwest in various places where excavations are in progress.

From the early sessions of the Pecos Conference, a chronological table of ancient life was evolved. For each period, tree-ring dates added chronology. The periods as decided upon at the Pecos Conference and the approximate times of their occurrence are as follows:

Pueblo V	—Recent
Pueblo IV	—1400 A.D.
Pueblo III	—1100 A.D.
Pueblo II } Pueblo I }	—Developmental Pueblo 950 A.D.
Basket Maker III	— 700 A.D.
Basket Maker II	— 400 A.D.
Basket Maker I	— 100 B.C. (?)

Several earlier misconceptions were corrected. The Basket Makers had indeed preceded the Pueblo people as Richard Wetherill had thought at first, but they were not different populations. The Basket Maker "long heads" and the Pueblo "broad heads" were not separate and distinct peoples. Later Pueblo mothers began to bind their babies to hard cradle boards which flattened the backs of their soft skulls. This custom produced the "broad heads" of later Pueblo times. Further excavations at Mesa Verde and at other Cliff Dweller sites showed that these people also were a part of the larger southwestern scheme. The Cliff Dwellers were simply Pueblo people who built their homes in cliffs either for defense or protection against the weather or both. Their masonry, their ceremonial rooms, their pottery, and other things they made and did showed them to be puebloan people like their neighbors.

This whole complex of southwestern life the Pecos conferees came to call "Anasazi." This is a Navajo word which Richard Wetherill had often used. It means "the ancient ones." The Navajos had often called Wetherill himself Anasazi because of his great interest in the ancient ones.

Although agriculture came from the south as early as several centuries before Christ, most of the Anasazi development took place after the birth of Christ. The main developments were in architecture and ceremonial life. The Anasazis apparently never felt the need for a calendar or a glyphic system of writing, but in architecture they were supreme. The peak of Anasazi development appeared in the Pueblo III Period or Golden Age. At this time, puebloan people built their towns from Colorado and Kansas in the north to the Mexican state of Chihuahua in the south. They lived as far west as Nevada and eastward into the Texas Panhandle. The greatest pueblo towns were at such places as Chaco Canyon in northwestern New Mexico and along the Little Colorado River in northern Arizona. Chaco Canyon is now a dry sandy wash with sandstone walls on either side. The Pueblo people built twelve great towns and some hundreds of smaller ones within ten miles along Chaco Canyon. One of the most famous of the Chaco apartment houses is called Pueblo Bonito. Pueblo Bonito is built of finely shaped stone masonry laid dry. It covers three acres of ground and contains over 800 rooms. It was four stories high in part and contained within its structures not only rows of rooms for every function but circular ceremonial kivas as well. Until a larger apartment house was built in New York in 1882, Pueblo Bonito and some of the other pueblo buildings were the largest communal buildings ever built in North or South America. In its heyday, around 1000 A.D., Pueblo Bonito housed some 1,500 inhabitants. Some time around 1100 A.D., the inhabitants of Pueblo Bonito and the other towns in Chaco Canyon simply abandoned these handsome structures.

But at the height of its glory, the ceremonial kivas of Pueblo Bonito hummed with ritual activity. The excavators there have found carved altars, painted stone slabs, and petroglyphs showing the rituals which the Indians practiced. We can gain some idea of their elaborate costumes and the equally elaborate dances from the practices of present-day Pueblo Indians. The rain ceremonies and healing ceremonies which they enact are undoubtedly similar to those which were practiced by the Chaco pueblo dwellers of a thousand years ago.

Even in Pueblo IV times, the Anasazi were still great. There had been great movements and disturbances. The Chaco towns were abandoned. The Mesa Verde cliff dwellings were deserted. Most of the other great pueblos, of which there were literally thousands to the north, were also deserted by their inhabitants. In places there is evidence of warfare but mostly the great communal dwellings seem to have been abandoned quite peaceably and for other reasons. New and even larger towns were established along the Rio Grande River. In the south, also, in what is now the state of Chihuahua in Old Mexico, the pueblo way of life was still carried on. Some of the largest pueblos of the Anasazi development were built during Pueblo IV times. Such a gigantic pueblo town was Sepawe near El Rito, New Mexico. Sepawe has never been excavated but, judging from the ruined walls on its surface, it probably contains more than 6,000 rooms and kivas.

But forces of disintegration and degeneration were already present in the Pueblo IV period. The tree rings tell that a great drought occurred from 1276 to 1299. It probably was this which caused much of the change and the abandonment of Mesa Verde. The disastrous drought undoubtedly shook the faith of the Anasazis in their deities. Certainly during Pueblo IV times, the Anasazi way of life was already in a decline.

It was at about this time that a number of predatory Indians called the Athabaskans moved in from the north. These Athabaskans, later to be called the Navajo and Apache, moved southward from centers which may have been as far north as northwestern Canada and Alaska. The Navajo and the Apache did not at first plant corn and beans and squash, nor did they build great communal buildings. Rather, they were a seminomadic and warlike people. Some of the pueblo towns fell victim to these invaders. In turn, the Navajo and Apaches learned ceremonies and practices from their Pueblo enemies. The Pueblo women had long woven beautiful blankets out of native cotton yarn. The Navajo learned to make striped blankets from the Pueblos. Today the Navajo weave these beautiful blankets for the tourist trade, while the Pueblos have lost the art almost entirely. The Apaches, too, picked up ceremonies from their Pueblo neighbors and even traded with them.

But it is doubtful whether the death of the Anasazi way of life was due entirely to the Athabaskan invaders or to drought. The causes of the decline of this civilization were complex and probably much like the causes which have brought about the fall of other great civilizations.

At the Pecos conferences, certain archaeologists began

to report a considerable amount of archaeological evidence of people in central and southern Arizona who were certainly not Anasazi. They proposed to call these southern Arizonans of long ago "Hohokam," which is a Pima Indian word meaning "those who have vanished." The Hohokam had started to practice agriculture and to erect buildings quite as early as the Anasazi. They never, however, built great apartment houses. Instead, the Hohokam built individual earthen lodges, often grouped around a plaza.

The greatest Hohokam town was called "Snaketown," by the excavators. It lies some 12 miles southwest of Chandler, Arizona. The ancient inhabitants of Snaketown had irrigated the almost completely arid surroundings with canals. At Snaketown archaeologists discovered a number of levels of Hohokam development. While the Anasazi were evolving from Basket Maker to early Pueblo to late Pueblo, the Hohokam also were developing a civilization which passed through several stages. During all of these stages, the Hohokam houses were earthen lodges. As the centuries passed, the form of these lodges changed. These people of southern Arizona had a golden age which was comparable to that of the great Anasazi centers to the north and east.

Actually the high point of the Hohokam civilization was not brought about through the works of the Hohokam alone. The greatest development at Snaketown and at other Hohokam centers was caused by an actual invasion of Anasazi people and Anasazi traits. It was these newcomers, called the "Salado" people, who came from Anasazi centers in New Mexico and who began to build in the Hohokam area thick-walled multistoried communal houses of adobe. These massive buildings were Anasazi rather than Hohokam. Much of the Hohokam tradition in pottery and ceremonialism was carried on during this fusion. It is interesting to note that the amalgamation of the Hohokam and the Anasazi seems to have been a peaceful one.

The Hohokam people of southern Arizona had closer connections with Old Mexico than the Anasazi had. Copper bells and other objects actually traded from Old Mexico are fairly common finds in Hohokam excavations. More remarkable were the ball courts which appeared early in the Hohokam civilization and have been found at almost all large Hohokam sites. The ball court and the ball game which was played on it were certainly Mexican. Ball courts appear at both Mexican and Mayan sites. In Old Mexico, the ball game was ceremonial rather than purely for sport. At Snaketown, a very large ball court was found by the excavators. At either end of the court, some 200 feet in length, were stones set in the hard caliche floor to serve as goals. In one Hohokam site, a rubber ball was found buried in a jar. This rubber ball, for use on the ball courts, must have been traded through intermediate tribes all the way from southern Mexico where wild rubber occurs.

Ancient Snaketown, with its impressive ball court and earthen lodges, is another example of the high state of culture achieved in the American Southwest. Here, in this semiarid country, many people had worked out civilized ways of life. Thousands of Hohokam and Anasazi had built buildings, and evolved ceremonial religions. They left traces of their doings in many places in this fascinating land, and only a fraction of the existing Hohokam and Anasazi ruins have been excavated by the probing shovel of the archaeologist. With future excavations, diggers will find out more about these ancient ways of life. Even with the evidence we can gain from the lives of the present-day Pueblo Indians, we have as yet discovered only a small part of the story of the prehistoric Southwest.

11

Eskimo Antiquity

THE AMERICAN INDIANS vary radically from one tribe to another. It is true that they are generally Mongoloid, but within the limits of these racial characteristics the different tribes of American Indians vary widely. When Europeans first discovered the New World continents, they found these different kinds of American Indians living in every part of America and in every kind of climate which is found in America. Numbers of European scientists have remarked upon the fact that American Indians occupied the unfavorable as well as the favorable parts of America.

Among the heterogeneous tribes of Indians and the different ways of life they lead, none is more striking than that of the Eskimos. On the face of the matter, the Eskimos live in an impossible place. It might be thought by people in temperate climates that no human beings could maintain life in the arctic wastes, and yet the Eskimos do just that. Furthermore, they seem to like it. Recently, when the United States government offered jobs in southern Alaska to Eskimos, most of the jobs were refused. The few Eskimos who did go to Juneau didn't like the warmer weather and the easier life there. They went back to the frozen north.

Under almost impossible conditions, the Eskimo has worked out a distinctive way of life. His weapons, his tools, even his art, are distinctive and like no other on the American continent. Physically, also, the Eskimo is easily recognizable. An Eskimo's skull, his teeth, and jaw are shaped differently from those of other American Indians. And yet the Eskimo is an Indian. His face and other physical characteristics identify him as a Mongoloid. However, a number of unmistakable characteristics set him apart.

Linguistically also, the Eskimo is distinct. Even though there are Eskimos from Alaska to Greenland—over 5,000 miles of coast line—the language of all these people is almost uniform. Indeed, a new song or a new joke introduced in Alaska will appear in Greenland at the other end of a long line of scattered Eskimo camps only about a year later. Of course, this is perhaps not remarkable as so many American Indians speak distinct tongues. And yet the Eskimo speech is very distinct and separate from the languages of other American Indians.

When anthropologists first began to study the Eskimos, they were struck by these distinctions. Ethnically, linguistically, and culturally the Eskimo is a law unto himself. Immediately the questions, "How old is this way of life? How long have people lived in the arctic wastes?" were asked.

When archaeologists first discovered that certain kinds of people lived in Europe during the last Ice Age, they wondered, of course, what had happened to these people and their way of life after the Ice Age passed. American archaeologists, too, thought that perhaps early Americans who had hunted Ice Age animals here during the glacial period might have wished to continue their way of life. Why could not some of these early Americans, they argued, have moved north with the retreating ice and continued their arctic hunting? Perhaps the Eskimos were descendants of the very first American hunters.

When scientists began to study the Eskimos and their way of life, this theory was seen to be impossible. The Eskimo maintains himself almost entirely by hunting sea mammals. Most of the hunting is done on the ice or in the water from a boat. Eskimo hunting is highly specialized and requires special equipment. On the other hand, our early American hunters tracked land mammals such as bison and mammoth. These two kinds of hunting are worlds apart.

A number of archaeologists at first thought that the Eskimos were simply other American Indians who had moved out to the arctic coast and taken up an Eskimo way of life. This easy explanation does not conform with the facts as we know them. The main stumbling block is that no other American Indians knew how to make the equipment without which it is impossible to survive on the arctic coast. If these first intrepid Indians had not had these vital implements, how could they have survived the first winter?

Eskimo life is impossible without two major items. These are the toggle-headed harpoon and the Eskimo lamp. The harpoon is a contrivance especially developed for the killing and retrieving of sea mammals. The seal, the walrus, and the whale of arctic waters may be killed with a spear or with a modern rifle, for that matter. However, with any ordinary weapon the body of the animal killed could not be retrieved. The stricken seal or walrus would simply sink and the hunter would go hungry. The toggle-headed harpoon is a special kind of spear with a detachable head. Not only is the pointed head detachable but it acts as a toggle. The point is fitted with a spur so that once the weapon is thrust deep into a seal or walrus, the spur turns the head sideways. The shaft of the harpoon, with which the cast was made, floats free and is retrieved by the hunter. A stout line is attached to a hole in the toggle-head of the harpoon. As the toggle-head is buried deep in the flesh of the stricken animal, this line is attached to a large float. Thus when the animal dies, the hunter retrieves the float and hauls up the line with the dead seal or walrus at the other end. With the toggle-headed harpoon, a skillful Eskimo hunter seldom loses his quarry.

The Eskimo lamp is a shallow dishlike receptacle usually cut from stone. Most Eskimo lamps are carved in the shape of a half circle with a small ledge on the side of the dish. The hollow of the receptacle is filled with oil from a sea mammal. The small ledge accommodates a wick of twisted moss. The oil in the dish is readily sucked up by the dry moss. The end of the wick is lighted and the oil burns with a hot sputtering flame. The Eskimo lamp provides light and heat. Light is very important throughout the long dark months of the arctic winter, and heat is a necessity without which human beings could not survive. It is important to remember also that the only fuel the Eskimo lamp can use is oil from the body of a sea mammal. It will not work with the tallow from land mammals such as caribou.

The toggle-headed harpoon and the Eskimo lamp are both complicated instruments which are useful only in the arctic. They could not have been invented any place else, and yet without them no group of human explorers could have survived even one season in that inhospitable place.

There are Eskimos on the arctic shores of Siberia, but most Eskimos live on the arctic littoral of North America and Greenland. The center of Eskimo activity lies in the vicinity of Hudson Bay. But in all of this territory, the first explorers could find no evidence of great antiquity. There were, it is true, hundreds of abandoned villages along the arctic coast. Even the early explorers, seeking the Northwest Passage, remarked upon the great number of deserted Eskimo habitations on bleak northern shores. But this was explained by the fact that the Eskimos, whose livelihood depended on the taking of seal with their toggle-headed harpoons, change the locations of their villages to better hunting grounds as the seal population followed the movements of fish. So abandoned villages were not necessarily traces of antiquity. Indeed, in the middle 1920s, most archaeologists were certain that the Eskimo way of life was not ancient at all and extended back, at most, only a few hundred years.

During the 1920s, Dr. Aleš Hrdlička was working in the Aleutian Islands. Primarily a physical anthropologist, he was also interested in the Aleutian island chain as a possible route of entry for Asiatics into North America. He was also intrigued by the physical differences between the Eskimos and their cousins the Aleuts and other American Indians.

One day during the short Alaskan summer, Dr. Hrdlička was working with a group of students far out in the Aleutian chain. A group of Eskimos paddled up to the beach where the scientists were gathered. Two of these Eskimos walked up to Dr. Hrdlička. They had heard that a great American scientist was working there. They had brought him some things, fragments of dark-colored ivory. The ivory was fossil walrus ivory, brown in color and obviously very old. But the objects were far more interesting than the material or its color. There were toggle-headed harpoon heads, knife-handles, foreshafts, and swivel-like objects all carved from the brownish red ivory. All the surfaces of these objects were decorated with beautiful oval and circular designs which flowed gracefully over their contours. Dr. Hrdlička had never seen any harpoon heads or other implements such as these before, nor had he ever seen artistic designs such as these in the north. The implements which the Eskimos had brought were obviously not modern. The ivory from which they were made was fossilized and had been buried in frozen ground for a very long time. Where had they found these things? The Eskimos said that they had been walrus hunting on St. Lawrence Island in the middle of the Bering Sea. On St. Lawrence Island, high above the beach, they had found a village where the ancients had lived. In the house pits of the village they had picked up the harpoon heads and other things. The Eskimos added that these things are not like those made by modern Eskimos. Dr. Hrdlička recognized this at a glance. When he returned that fall to the National Museum in Washington, he told his colleagues of the find and brought back the ivory objects as samples.

Dr. Henry Collins, Jr., also of the National Museum, sailed to the Far North in 1931. He landed on St. Lawrence Island with an excavating crew and digging equipment. Eskimo hunters showed the archaeologists the ancient village in which they had found the house pits and fossil ivory.

In a few weeks of exploration, Collins and his party found several dozen more ancient villages. The whole shore line of St. Lawrence Island was dotted with the saucer-shaped depressions where houses had been dug into the frozen turf. And around these ancient villages were piles of debris containing the bones of walrus, seal, and occasionally whale, and also thousands of objects left by the ancient Eskimos who had lived there.

The archaeologists called the people who had lived on the shores of St. Lawrence Island the "Old Bering Sea People." Digging was difficult in the frozen tundra and sludge of the village site. Half-frozen water seeped into the excavations. Mud and slime covered everything, including the excavators themselves. During the short arctic summer, the archaeologists worked feverishly to recover the story of the Old Bering Sea People. It was a fascinating one.

The Old Bering Sea hunters had been Eskimos, and no simple Eskimos either. They had made beautifully carved harpoon heads. They had used Eskimo lamps to warm their houses. Their houses had been dug partly into the frozen ground for protection. They were built of timbers, whale ribs, and whale jaws. The floors were paved with stone. The doorways were narrow tunnels through which the people crawled to enter. The Old Bering Sea People had worked industriously to gather the sparse driftwood which was brought that far north on the ocean currents. The houses themselves were cleverly constructed to combat the terrible cold of the arctic winter. Most important of all, the Old Bering Sea People had the two essential Eskimo implements, the harpoon and the lamp.

The Old Bering Sea hunters had thousands of tools and utensils which made this arctic life possible and even pleasant. They hunted seal, walrus, and sometimes whale. Birds were killed with bows and arrows or with small spears launched from a wooden spear thrower. Fish, principally cod, were caught with hooks of wood and bone. They made knives and projectile points of chipped flint and ground slate. They had snow shovels, ice picks, and mattocks. From walrus ivory they made bone needles, needle cases, and ladles. To keep out the glare of summer sun on snow and ice, they carved ivory goggles with narrow slits to protect their eyes. For difficult travel on ice, they carved ice creepers of bone or ivory which were attached to the soles of their boots. For hunting and travel over the treacherous Bering Sea, they had skin-covered boats like the modern kayak. They also built a large double-ended open boat called an umiak. Although they had dogs, they did not use them for pulling their small sledges. The Old Bering Sea Eskimos pulled toboggans and sledges by hand. Perhaps the most remarkable thing about all of these tools and utensils was the fact that most of them were decorated in a beautiful and artistic way. Even in the midst of their struggle for existence, these Eskimos had had time to carve and engrave their harpoon points and sledge runners. They had decorated almost everything they made in their characteristic way.

After careful study, the archaeologists concluded that the Old Bering Sea Eskimo culture was well established on St. Lawrence Island by the time of Christ. Patently also, this was no simple Eskimo culture. If anything, the Old Bering Sea way of life was more complex and produced a greater variety of implements and objects than that of the modern Eskimo. The Old Bering Sea villages on St. Lawrence Island showed very plainly that the Eskimo way of life had been going on for a very long time.

Where had the Old Bering Sea People and their fully developed Eskimo culture come from? It seemed to the scientists working on the problem that the answer lay across the few miles of open water which separates St. Lawrence Island from the Siberian shore. They felt that Eskimos from Siberia had come first to St. Lawrence Island and thence to Alaska itself.

Sure enough, Old Bering Sea villages were found on the Siberian coast as well as on the coast of Alaska. When the archaeologists returned to St. Lawrence Island for further excavation during the short summers, they found out more and more about these people. On other islands and around the periphery of the Bering Sea they found more and more ancient arctic villages. It became clear that the Old Bering Sea Eskimos had ruled all of these northern shores in the early centuries of the Christian era. They had moved from village to village in their kayaks and umiaks and had hunted the open seas. Certainly, when these civilizations were at a height, the population of these arctic islands and coasts was larger than it is today.

The archaeologists continued to look for some earlier form of Eskimo life from which the Old Bering Sea culture might have developed. In the ancient village of Okvik on the northern Alaska shores, they found a likely candidate. The village houses were round and built partly underground to keep out the cold. As the archaeologists dug first one Okvik house and then another, they recovered thousands of implements just as they had done in the Old Bering Sea villages. As the Okvik middens are overlaid by typical Old Bering Sea debris, it was obvious that the Okvik people had lived in Alaska and northeastern Siberia even before the Old Bering Sea Eskimos. Russian archaeologists found Okvik villages on East Cape in Siberia in 1951. But the Okvik was not a simple culture either. The harpoon heads, the bird darts, the multibarbed fishhooks and chipped or ground knives and drills were all beautifully made. The Okvik had almost as many kinds of weapons and utensils as the Old Bering Sea people. Okvik craftsmen also carved bone and ivory into abstract designs with great skill. Indeed, as the archaeologists studied the things that the Okvik people had left behind more closely, it became apparent that the Old Bering Sea way of life had grown directly out of the Okvik. An earlier culture had been found, but archaeologists had yet to find the original Eskimos who had invented the complicated toggle-headed harpoon and who first thought of the principle of the Eskimo lamp.

And constantly as the archaeologists sought for Eskimo beginnings, signs and indications pointed to Siberian shores. Almost certainly the Okvik had come from Asia. In Siberia, perhaps, the secret of Eskimo origins lay.

In trying to learn about the culture and origin of the Eskimos, archaeologists and explorers found many other villages. At Ipiutak on the shores of the Arctic Ocean near Point Hope, Dr. Helge Larsen, a Scandinavian archaeologist, in 1948 dug an enormous site containing 800 dwellings arranged in five long avenues. The houses were typically Eskimo, built of driftwood logs supplemented with stones and moss and partly beneath the surface of the ground. The Ipiutak hunters killed seal, walrus, and fish. They went far inland to hunt caribou when the herds migrated. The really remarkable aspect of the Ipiutak is that the several thousand inhabitants of this tremendous town were able to derive enough food from the surrounding terrain to feed themselves.

As with the other cultures, the Ipiutak was not a simple or primitive way of life. On the contrary, Ipiutak art is the most elaborate and distinctive of all the Eskimo styles. Ipiutak artisans decorated everything they made with graceful combinations of circles, curved lines, spurs, and parallel motifs. They carved from walrus ivory wonderful animal forms and curious spiral ivory swivels of unknown use. The bodies of some of the very important Ipiutak dead were equipped with carved inlaid eyeballs of ivory. Some skeletons were provided with carved nose plugs of ivory. Others had elaborate decorated ivory mouthpieces.

The art style of the Ipiutak, elaborate as it is, is related to that of the Old Bering Sea Eskimos. Their implements and weapons are also similar although distinctive. Certainly some of the Old Bering Sea villages on St. Lawrence Island were occupied at the same time as the great Ipiutak town on Point Hope.

As early as 1925, a discovery was made which promised to solve the mystery of the origin of the Eskimos. This find did not take place on some lonely arctic shore but in the basement of the Canadian National Museum, where Dr. Diamond Jenness was working over some old collections that had been sent from the arctic years before. The Canadian National Museum is like many such institutions in being behind with its unpacking and cataloguing. Many of these collections were still in their original crates. Dr. Jenness noticed some Eskimo harpoon heads which were smaller and cruder than any he had seen before. These artifacts had been sent to the Canadian Museum years before from Cape Dorset near Hudson Bay on the arctic coast.

Dr. Jenness went there to investigate. Other archaeologists too examined these lonely shores for ancient villages of the very earliest Eskimos. There were scattered villages along the bleak coasts. The Dorset culture, as it came to be called, was an Eskimo culture quite distinct from those of Alaska far to the west. Dorset Eskimos had centered around Hudson Bay but also lived in scattered villages in Baffinland, Ellesmere Island, northern Greenland, Labrador, and even as far south as Newfoundland. The archaeologists soon discovered many indications that throughout these scattered villages the Dorset Eskimos had lived in the eastern arctic as early as the time of Christ.

Perhaps the answer was here. The Eskimo way of life may have come from the east. The toggle-headed harpoon and the Eskimo lamp were perhaps the invention of some early people in eastern Canada or even New England.

Excavations among the villages of the Dorset Eskimos did seem to show that this was the crudest and most primitive Eskimo culture yet discovered. The Dorsets had lived in circular houses built partly underground and constructed from materials they could find on the spot, such as driftwood, or stone, or sod blocks. The Dorset houses were sloppily made although snug enough to serve their purpose. The Dorset Eskimos lived by hunting sea mammals and birds and by fishing. They also ate birds' eggs and berries and other foods they could find during the arctic summers.

The Dorset Eskimos knew the toggle-headed harpoon but had a very crude version of it. Their harpoon heads were fitted with rough rectangular sockets. The holes for the harpoon line were gouged instead of drilled. Apparently the Dorsets were the only early Eskimos who did not know or use the drill. Indeed, the Dorsets did not have the bow and arrow, at least at first. Possibly they did not have the common types of Eskimo boats or the dog sled. They did use the Eskimo lamp, but their lamps were crudely hollowed-out boulders and roughly made.

In artistic attainment also, the Dorset Eskimos were the poorest of the northern artisans. They decorated their harpoon heads and other utensils with only a few parallel lines and hashures. Many of their implements were not decorated at all. One has the distinct impression that the Dorset Eskimos were too busy wresting their existence from the arctic wastes to bother with such frivolities as art.

In vain archaeologists searched the coasts of Labrador and Hudson Bay for some very early Eskimo village which might prove to be the beginning of the Dorset way of life. They did not find one. On the contrary, the Dorset Eskimo towns which the archaeologists found were contemporaneous with or later than the Old Bering Sea habitations. Nothing in the Dorset area seemed to be as early as the Okvik on the shores of the Bering Sea. In fact, many of the Dorset villages were obviously quite late in time. In some places the Dorset way of life had lingered until as late as a thousand years after Christ. It became obvious that, instead of being the original Eskimo culture from which all others had sprung, the Dorset was a benighted offshoot of the original culture. Perhaps the great expanse of Hudson Bay had been a major barrier to the spread of Eskimo civilization. The Dorsets were far eastern country cousins of the Okvik, Old Bering Sea, and Ipiutak. It was in the far west of the arctic coast that the Eskimo way of life began and developed to the furthest point. The Eskimo way of life had come from Siberia. This must have occurred at least a thousand years before Christ.

The harpoon and the Eskimo lamp must have been invented somewhere on the Siberian coast in a primitive Eskimo village. The Eskimos and the Eskimo way of life came over from Siberia long after the first Sandia and Folsom hunters had crossed that way.

But human beings are the most ingenious of all the mammals. They can survive where any other mammal would perish. And survive they did. The amazing thing is that the Eskimo way of life is not only possible but the Eskimos like it. They have time to develop art, social life, and games. Their religion is most elaborate. Far from being grim, the Eskimos are the happiest of people. During the long dark arctic winters they travel along the sea ice with their dog sleds to go visiting. It is remarkable that a way of life which produces complete human satisfaction is based upon a harpoon and a lamp.

12

The Mathematical Mayas

WHEN the Spanish conqueror, Cortes, had gained glory and gold in the Valley of Mexico, he had aroused the envy of every adventuresome caballero of the times. Stories reached the Spanish colony of Cuba that there were other mighty cities to be conquered and gold to be gained. The first white men had reached the land of the Mayas as early as 1511. In that year a caravel commanded by a Spanish official named Valdivia foundered on some shoals off the coast of Yucatán. Seven men died of thirst but the surviving twelve reached the Yucatán mainland, only to be captured by the Mayas. All but two, including Valdivia, died or were killed and eaten as human sacrifices by the Indians. The two survivors joined the Mayas and learned their language. In 1517 and again in 1518, Spanish ships skirted the shores of the Mayan area, lured there by persistent stories of gold and treasure. In 1519, Cortes himself led an expedition to Yucatán where he rescued one of the survivors from the ill-fated Valdivia expedition. The other survivor, a man named Guerrero, had married a Mayan woman and refused to leave his family. From these castaways came tales of great cities in the Yucatán jungles. The cities were built of stone. There were tall terraced pyramids with ornate temples on their summits. There were gold and precious stones, too, it was said, and great treasure houses far surpassing any that Cortes and his followers found in the Valley of Mexico.

It was inevitable, then, that a Spanish expedition should be fitted out to fight its way into these cities, take this treasure, and convert the heathen Indians to Catholicism. Francisco de Montejo, who had been with Cortes during the reconnaissance of 1518, headed the expedition. There were two Montejos, father and son. Both of these Spanish dons undoubtedly considered themselves fortunate men to lead an expedition into the treasure houses of the Mayas of Yucatán. Every soldier in their little army dreamed of the riches he would soon possess. In the Valley of Mexico there had been only one wealthy city, Tenochtitlán; while in the Mayan jungles there were a dozen such spectacular cities, each one full of gold and precious jewels. Further, there were thousands of new heathen souls to be saved for the church. This, indeed, was to be the most glorious expedition the world had ever seen.

Montejo and his army of soon-to-be-rich conquistadores landed on the shores of Yucatán in 1527. As they pressed into the jungles of the Yucatán Peninsula, they found many Mayas. The Indians fought fiercely with their primitive weapons. Curiously enough, the Mayas were aided by Guerrero, the Spanish castaway of the Valdivia expedition, who cast his lot with them. Perhaps because of the knowledge which the Spanish renegade furnished his Indian allies, the fighting went badly for Spain in spite of the Spanish arms and armor. Many Spaniards fell beneath the obsidian-tipped spears and stone-edged clubs of the Mayan warriors. But the Spanish soldiers fighting for gold and their church pressed forward.

Montejo and his army gained some victories. They captured some Mayan cities and they saw other friendly centers which they did not need to capture. The Spanish conquerors noted, almost in passing, that most of the Mayan centers were already abandoned and crumbling into ruins. There were stone pyramids and ornate pyramid temples, but over most of these the jungle vegetation had already begun to grow. Even in the centers and cities where the Mayan Indians still lived, there was an air of decay. The Mayan armies which opposed the conquerors came from small grass huts and not from the ruined cities. And, worst of all, there was no treasure. There were only a few baubles of gold and jade. Montejo thought that the crafty Mayas had hidden their gold and treasures before the Spanish could get to them. And so he pressed farther and farther into the center of the Yucatán jungle.

The fall of Montezuma's city of Tenochtitlán in the Valley of Mexico had been swift and the rewards for the Spanish very great. The expedition of the Montejos dragged on and on and on. Many of the Spanish soldiers became disillusioned and straggled back to Cuba and Spain. Most of the adventurers of the first army fell beneath the arrows of the Mayas. A second army, organized by the Montejos, attempted to enter Yucatán from the other side, from the west. The Mayan Empire may have been crumbling and near its end, but that did not lessen the fierceness of the Mayan warriors. Expedition after expedition failed and, worst of all, when after almost twenty years of expeditions, the Spanish finally subdued the Mayas, they discovered what Montejo must have guessed long before. The Spanish had not conquered an empire in its full bloom and at the height of its wealth. The Spanish armies had overcome the ghost of a great people and there was little gold. Disillusioned, most of them wounded and none of them wealthy, those Spaniards who came out of the campaigns of Yucatán gave a very poor account of the Mayan country. Because of their disillusionment, they failed to see the glory of the great crumbling cities. They did not even record the existence of many of the magnificent Mayan centers which they must have marched through.

The churchmen who moved into Yucatán in the wake of the Spanish armies found thousands of heathen souls to be converted. This, at least, would be a great gain.

The Christians began with characteristic fervor to destroy the remnants of pagan religion which opposed the acceptance of Christianity. As the Mayas had already abandoned most of their great religious centers, these presented no particular problem. The greatest obstacles to Christianity were the priests who still carried on the rites of their religion, and most especially the written books which the priests used in the determination of religious days and special festivals and in foretelling the future. The Christian bishops in charge of the conversion of the Mayan souls built great bonfires of pagan paraphernalia, including these wicked manuscripts. The enthusiasm of these early churchmen is understandable, but by burning these books they destroyed the products of thousands of years of Mayan civilization. The books were concerned with pagan gods, it is true, but they also contained the essence of Mayan thought and perhaps even Mayan history. These people had evolved a system of writing and a knowledge of mathematics as great as that of any other people in

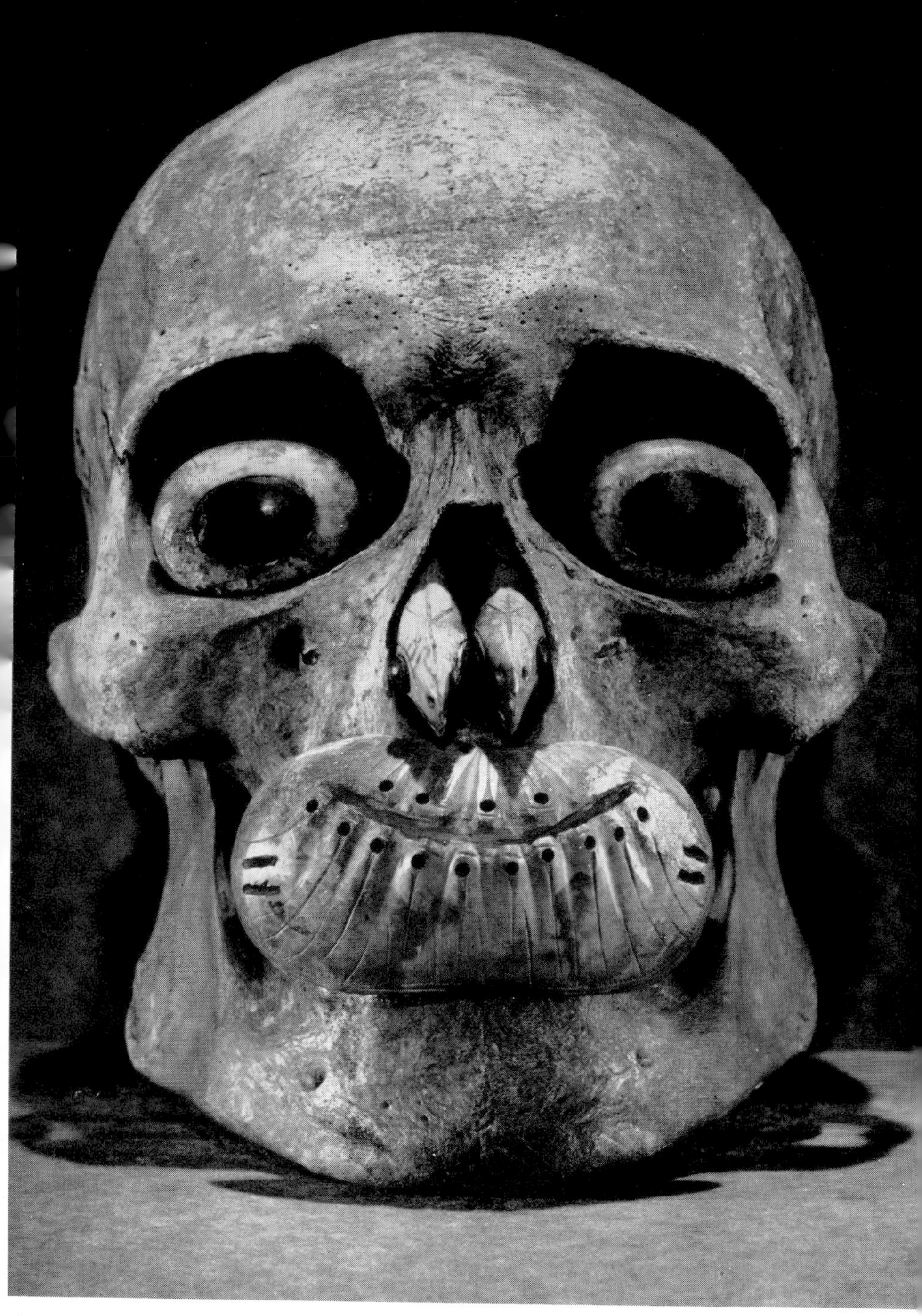

Plate 29. Skull with ivory eyes with inlaid pupils of jet, ivory nose plugs finely carved to represent birds' heads, and ivory mouth cover. Buried city of Ipiutak, northwest Alaska.

Plate 30. Model of an Aztec temple. Mexico.

Plate 31. Aerial view of the Pyramid of the Sun. Teotihuacán, Mexico.

Plate 32. Reproduction of Aztec calendar stone. Floor of the Solar Room of the Hayden Planetarium, New York City.

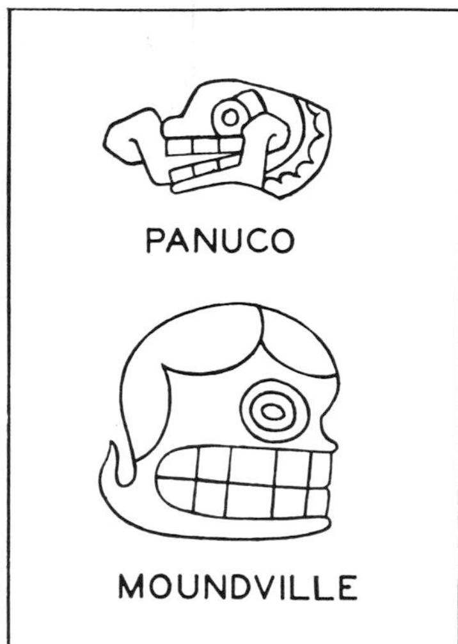

Plate 33. Skull designs from southeastern United States and from Mexico.

Plate 34. Designs dealing with the apotheosis of warriors. From Mexico and southeastern United States.

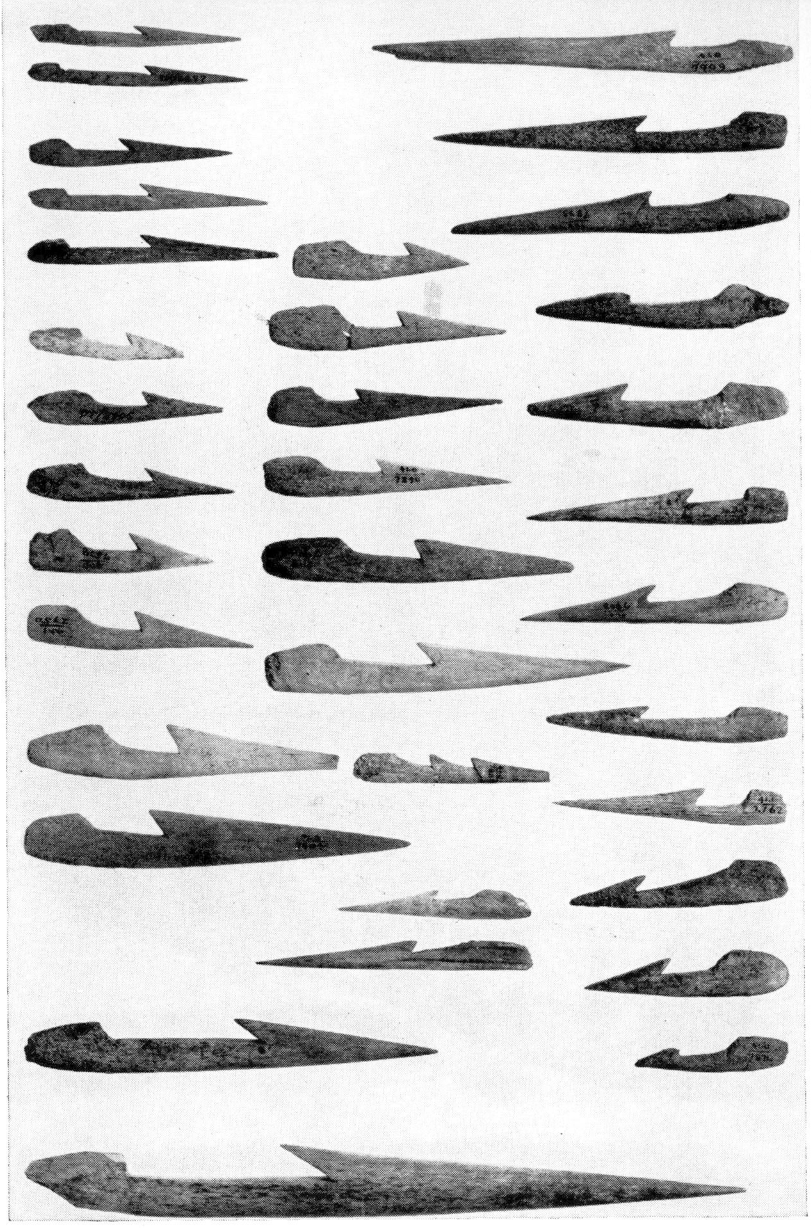

Plate 35. Harpoon points of different periods. Beagle Channel, Chile.

Plate 36. *Projectile and knife points of five cultural periods. Straits of Magellan.*

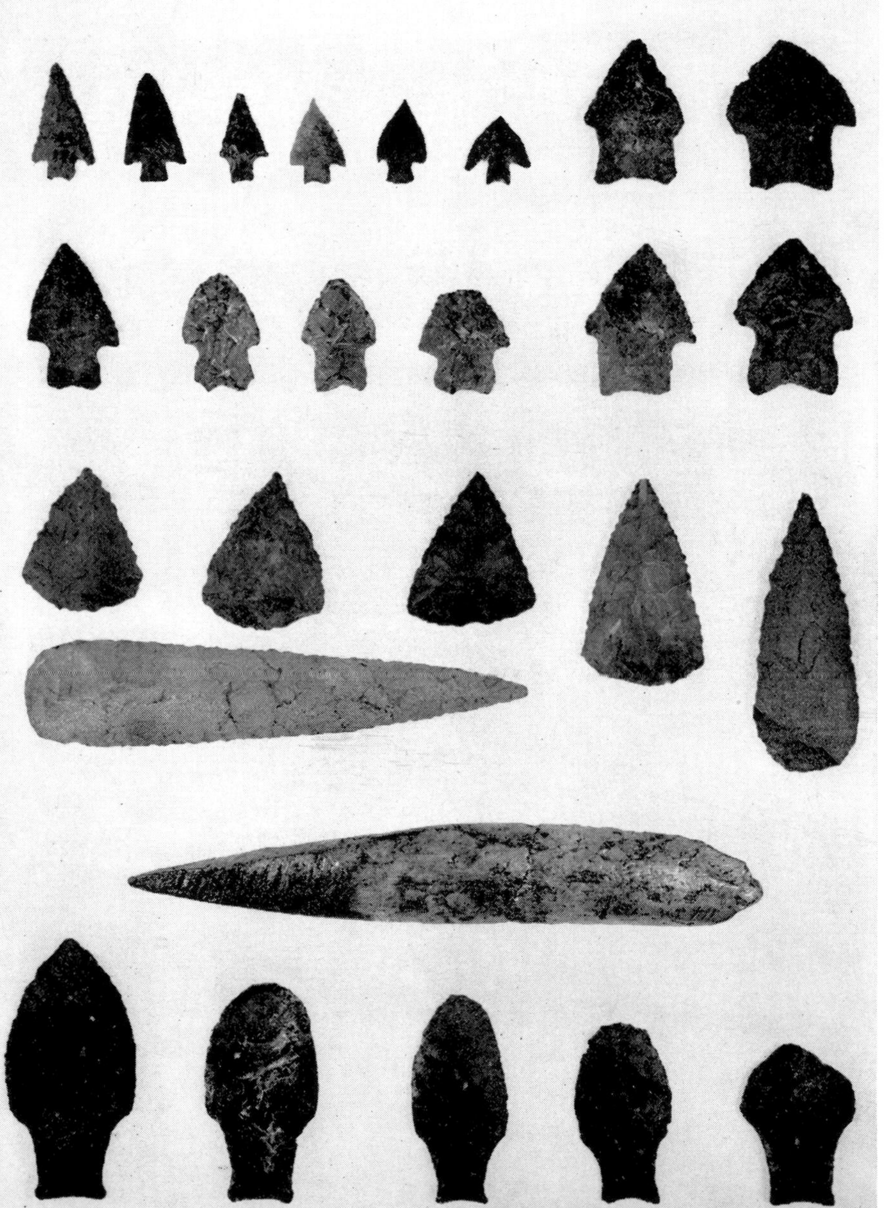

Plate 37. Cast of pottery dish with modeled human figure. Tiahuanaco style. Valley of Nazca, Peru.

Plate 38. Casts of modeled Nazca jars. Peru.

Plate 39. Ceremonial urn of Tiahuanaco Epigonal Period. Valley of Nazca, Peru.

Plate 40. Prehistoric cloth. Valley of Nazca, Peru.

Plate 41. One of the thirty figures on each side of the main figure of the Gateway to the Sun. Tiahuanaco, Peru.

Plate 42. Peruvian water jar. Coastal Tiahuanaco or Huasi style.

Plate 43. Painted polychrome Tiahuanaco cups. Peru.

Plate 44. A herd of gold llamas. Lake Titicaca, Peru.

Plate 45. Monolith. Tiahuanaco, Peru.

Plate 46. Aerial view of Chan Chan, capital of the Chimu Empire, Near Trijillo,

the New World. But the Christian clerics were blind to the importance of such accomplishments. The books were pernicious and so they destroyed them.

Bishop Landa, the second bishop of Mérida which was the center of Christian activities in Yucatán, is given credit for having directed most of the campaign of destruction. Actually, the campaign of burning and blotting out the Mayan culture had begun long before Bishop Landa's time. The good Bishop Landa was only casually interested in what the Mayan glyphs might mean. It is said that the alphabet which some of the Mayan scholars furnished Bishop Landa was deliberately false because they hated the Christian bishop and wished to mislead him. Certainly this alphabet produced gibberish. Christianity finished what time and the Spanish soldiers had already begun.

The destruction was not quite thorough. Three Mayan manuscripts escaped the fire of the zealots. These three books were carried back to Europe probably by Spanish soldiers as souvenirs. It is probable also that the possession of such books was expressly forbidden by the church. Since most of the great religious centers in the interior had been abandoned before the Montejo expedition, the very knowledge of the existence of these places was lost. The Spaniards destroyed other Mayan cities on the coast, usually by tearing down the ancient buildings and using the cut stone blocks to build churches and other modern structures. Bishops and enthusiastic friars in Yucatán converted the disorganized remnants of the Mayas to Christianity. A few stalwart Indians retreated into the jungles and kept up a semblance of their ancient rites, but their priests were gone and they had forgotten how to write or read the ancient glyphs and no longer understood the mathematical calculations. The ancient cities of the Mayas were abandoned and forgotten. The conquest of the empire of the Mayas had been, by and large, a bitter disappointment to the Spaniards. History forgot the incident. The Mayan land and the Mayan people sank into oblivion. It was 300 years before the Mayas were rediscovered.

John L. Stephens was an American diplomat and an amateur archaeologist. Stephens and an English artist, Robert Catherwood, were traveling in Central America and southern Mexico. Stephens had traveled in many parts of the world and written of his travels. In the early nineteenth century, when travel was difficult, such travelogues made very interesting reading and were extremely popular. Stephens was interested in people and places. Central America was a world unknown to Europe in the 1830s. So Stephens explored and wrote a book about his discoveries. He landed in Honduras in 1831. He wanted to see the cities and the people in the surrounding territories. When he heard that there were ancient ruins in the vicinity, he went to see them. He took Catherwood with him to sketch the places and antiquities which they might find. In this way Stephens rediscovered an empire which Europe had forgotten.

In the jungles of Honduras, the local Indians showed Stephens and Catherwood some carved stone monuments. With their hands the two men pulled vines and earth mold from the ancient carvings. Catherwood painstakingly copied the grotesque masked faces and glyphs which were carved in high relief on the stone pillars. The glyphs were unreadable, for the Indians who showed Stephens and Catherwood these glyphs no longer had any knowledge of their meaning.

Stephens and Catherwood found other carved stones and evidences of ancient life as they traveled farther into the jungles. In places there were massive stone walls and the half-disintegrated hulks of masonry pyramids. Atop the pyramids and around them were buildings also constructed of stone and stucco. These too were ornamented with grotesque masks and curious symbols. Stephens and Catherwood had by chance stumbled again upon the great ceremonial centers of the early Mayas. The carved stone pillars which Catherwood first copied were the Mayan stelae which had been set up on the occasion of the erection of a new pyramid or temple. Stephens was never able to read the glyphs which were carved on the face of the stelae. The revelation of those secrets remained for later scholars.

What Stephens did reveal was the romance of a lost civilization. Stephens' descriptions and Catherwood's illustrations of Mayan antiquities focused attention on these important pieces of lost American history. The history of Mayan archaeology really begins with the rediscovery by Stephens and Catherwood.

Archaeologists from the United States, Mexico, and a dozen European countries were attracted to the Mayan area. Excavations were begun at some of the sites which Stephens had described and at others which he never saw. Explorers penetrated farther into the jungles of Honduras, Guatemala, and Yucatán following reports of ruined pyramid cities brought out of the bush by the local "chicle" or chewing-gum gatherers. At the same time that more and more Mayan ceremonial centers were being plotted on the maps, scholars sought out the military accounts of the Montejos from the musty files of Spanish archives. The descriptions and accounts of Bishop Landa were again examined. Archaeologists never found a Rosetta Stone to solve the mystery of the Mayan glyphs. Scholars did it with a little information, much research, and pure reason.

It was obvious from the first that many of the carvings

on the Mayan stelae had to do with counting based on a "bar and dot system." A bar equaled 5 and a dot equaled 1. However, there seldom appeared more bars and dots than would equal the number 20. The bars and dots were almost always accompanied by glyphs, usually in the form of a grotesque face or mask. The counts in each case seemed to mean a certain number of mask symbols. The secret was, of course, the meaning of the mask symbols themselves.

If the Mayas had not been so mathematically minded, their system would never have been deciphered. As it was, the bar and dot counts and the mask symbols were soon demonstrated to be part of an elaborate calendar. The rediscovery of this calendar and its mathematical intricacies was not the work of any one scholar. Early in the twentieth century a dozen men worked out the meanings of the various glyphs.

Most of these scholars started with the writings of Bishop Landa, especially as contained in his account called the *Relación de las Cosas de Yucatán,* written at a time when a few Mayan priests still lived who could read hieroglyphic writing. When Landa wrote down the smattering of information he left to us, probably about 1566, the calendar was still in use. Landa even mentions that his chief source of information was one Nachi Cocon who, in his youth, had been a prince and priest familiar with the hieroglyphic writing and the calendric counts of his people. Bishop Landa scathingly denounces the whole calendar as the work of the devil but in spite of himself gave enough information so that later scholars could begin their complicated task. It is tantalizing to contemplate what information the worthy bishop might have passed down to us from the devil and Nachi Cocon had he asked a dozen pertinent questions and written down the answers.

Even today, with thousands of hours of research, only about one third of the Mayan hieroglyphs have been accurately deciphered. Most of this third deals with the calendar round. Since archaeologists are so concerned with time, this is perhaps the most important part.

Many of the Mayan glyphs which remain as yet undeciphered undoubtedly tell of religious matters and possibly of history. Few if any of the monuments seem to have been erected for personal glorification like those of the Egyptian and Mesopotamian kings. Rather, the events which were important to the Mayan rulers were the erection of the great pyramids and temples to their gods. In most Mayan monuments, the calendric notations are found in connection with other glyphs. Most of these are obviously the dates on which buildings and monuments were erected. So exact were the mathematical calculations of the Mayan priests that the dates which they recorded on these dedications could not possibly be confused with any other during the next 374,440 years, which is eternity as far as human life is concerned. By what kind of calculations had the ancient Mayan priests achieved accuracy of this sort?

First and foremost the earliest Mayas must have been astronomers. They observed the movements of the sun, the moon, the stars, and especially the planets. They soon determined that the solar year consisted of 365 days plus a fraction of a day. They divided this year into 18 months of 20 days each. At the end was an extra period of 5 days which came to be considered extremely unlucky. Each of these 19 periods was ruled over by a certain god who had certain attributes.

In addition to the solar year of 360 plus 5 days, the Mayas evolved a sacred year of 260 days which they called a *tzolkin* or "count of days." Actually this artificial ceremonial year was far more important to them than the solar year.

Each day of the 20-day month was given a separate name. From the records of Bishop Landa, scholars were able to determine the 20 name days and also the designations of the 18 months and the 5-day unlucky period at the end of the year. When a Maya was born, he was usually given the name of the day of his birth, and his patron saint was the guardian deity of that day.

In evolving this elaborate calendar, the ancient Mayan priests first determined that they would record only elapsed time, rather than current time as in our own system. Thus, when a Mayan calendric count noted the first day of the month Pop, they actually meant the second day. Also, these original mathematicians soon found that they needed a notation for zero. With a glyph to indicate zero, the Mayan priests evolved a calendric count which relied upon the position of the glyph signs as well as upon the meaning of each symbol. The common Mayan glyph for zero was a shell. Only two or three times in the history of the world was the concept of zero discovered. The Hindus of India discovered the principle of the zero. Of the two independent discoveries, that of the Maya was the earlier. The ancient Babylonians also invented a concept for zero even earlier than the Mayas or Hindus. The Babylonans reckoned sexagesimally with a unit of 60.

With the 365-day solar year, and the 260-day sacred year, and the 20-day month, the Mayan calendar was fairly simple. Into this simplicity, however, they introduced, for reasons unknown to us, the number 13, which was connected with each of the 20 name days in turn, as $13 \times 20 = 260$. It is obvious that the 260-day sacred year was derived from this calculation.

By combining the solar year and the sacred year, as two

periods of time which run concurrently, the Mayan mathematicians came out with the calculation of 18,980 days or 52 years. In other words, every 52 years, these two calendars returned to the same day on which they had started. The Aztecs, the Zapotecs, the Mixtecs, and other people of Central America and Mexico who derived their calendars from the Mayas, considered the 52-year period as the most important count of years. None of these other people ever went beyond the 52-year calculation. For the Mayas, however, it was only the beginning.

The entire Maya calendar is really vigesimal, or based upon the number 20. The only exception to this is the 18 months plus 5 extra days which go to make up the 365 days of the solar year. Other than this, everything in the Mayan count is divisible by 20. So accurate were they in these calculations that they often recorded a calculation of 23,040,000,000 days, a fantastic period of time even by modern standards. They wanted to make absolutely sure that the date which they wrote on their monuments could never be misconstrued.

The Mayan calendar was usually recorded with the elapsed day or "kin" as the basic unit in this system:

20 kins = 1 uinal or month of 20 days
18 uinals = 1 tun or year of 360 days
20 tuns = 1 katun of 7,200 days
20 katuns = 1 baktun or cycle of 144,000 days
20 baktuns = 1 pictun or 2,880,000 days
20 pictuns = 1 calabtun or 57,600,000 days
20 calabtuns = 1 kinchiltun or 1,152,000,000 days
20 kinchiltuns = 1 alautun or 23,040,000,000 days

For practical purposes, however, the Mayan chronologists usually wrote dates beginning with a cycle or baktun of 144,000 days. Since they wrote each date with the glyphs in a certain position, it is easy for modern scholars to read a Mayan date. "Long count" dates of the so-called initial series, were usually recorded first. A typical date would be 9.17.0.0.0. Such a date meant that 9 periods of 144,000 days, 17 periods of 7,200 days, no periods of 360 days, no periods of 20 days, and no periods of 1 day had elapsed since the point at which the whole calendar had begun.

What was not known was the point at which these ancient calculators had begun their calendar. We date our own calendar from the birth of Christ and count backwards or forwards from that point. Obviously the Mayan priests also had a fixed date which they considered to be the beginning of recorded time. The zero date of Mayan chronology was a certain "4 ahau, 8 cumhu." This mythological date occurred some 3,400 years before the earliest dated Mayan monument which has been found. We can only guess that this beginning point was derived from something important which occurred 3,000 years before Mayan records were carved on stone. The earliest recorded Mayan dates were already in the seventh baktun and most were later than that.

In addition to the mathematical calculations of this fabulous calendar, the Mayas had evolved two glyphs for each time period. They also noted on most monuments a so-called "secondary series," which was a formula by which the calendric correction for leap year was made. Considering that they had no telescopes or sextants or any other exact instruments with which to measure the movement of the heavenly bodies, it is astounding that these corrections were conceived of at all.

Besides the leap-year corrections, the Mayan priests noted a supplementary series, or moon count. This notation of glyphs and bar and dot symbols usually followed the "long count" of the initial series as though to make absolutely certain that there could be no mistake about the amount of elapsed time which was being recorded. Certainly no modern mathematician dealing with astrophysics was ever more thorough about his calculations than the Mayan priest of ten centuries ago.

Perhaps the greatest achievement of any people in ancient America were the Mayan calendar counts and the calculations with which they were kept. The most outstanding examples of these calculations are to be found, not on the stone monuments, but in the three Mayan manuscripts which escaped the destructive enthusiasm of the Christians. These three are the Codex Dresdensis, the Codex Tro-Cortesianus, and the Codex Peresianus.

Each of these three books consisted of long strips of paper made from pulp pounded from the bark of a tree. They were folded like a screen. A wash of fine white paint was applied to both sides of the bark-paper strips to supply an adequate background for the glyphs and numbers inscribed on their surfaces. The painting was done carefully in several shades of red, blue, yellow, brown, green, and a shiny black. Each of these three Mayan books deals with religious matters, horoscopes, and the calendar. Unfortunately not one of them deals with history, science, or architecture. Any books of this kind which might have existed have been destroyed.

One of the three, the Codex Dresdensis turned up in Vienna in 1739 where it had probably been brought or sent by some Spanish soldier, possibly even Montejo himself. The Dresden Codex, so-called because it was later presented to the librarian of the royal library in Dresden, is considered the highest intellectual achievement of the New World. In this book are the mathematical calculations of a very mathematically minded people. If only the

Dresden book remained to us and we knew nothing of the Mayan cities themselves, we would still have an insight into the keen minds of ancient scholars whose very names have been forgotten.

From the dates carved upon Mayan monuments, it has been possible to unravel much of their history. Archaeologists have found that the Mayan civilization began in what is now Guatemala, especially in the area around Lake Petén. Several dozen great ceremonial centers in the Lake Petén district and in neighboring Honduras contain most of the early Mayan dated stelae and monuments. Actually the very earliest Mayan dates which have been found are carved upon small objects such as the jade plaque known as the Leyden Plate, and their exact place of discovery cannot now be determined. The long-count dates of the Petén cities break off at the even date 10.3.0.0.0. Why this is so has never been determined. Recent excavations at the great Petén city of Tikal may reveal the secret of this sudden ending. The group of Mayan ceremonial centers in this area is usually called the Old Empire. The Old Empire may have come to such an abrupt end because of a pestilence, agricultural failure, drought, or moral disintegration.

Whatever the reasons, they must have been very important ones, for the people who had built these great ceremonial cities abandoned them and moved northward. They streamed down out of the highlands of Guatemala in two main routes of migration which have been called "The Great Descent" and "The Lesser Descent." As the people moved out of the hills and onto the Yucatán plains, they stopped in favorable places and built new ceremonial cities. Some of these Middle Empire cities are great in their own right. The architecture of the temples had changed to some extent. There were new kinds of stucco masks and different methods of stone carvings. But essentially the life was the same. The Mayan priests still kept the calendric calculations and carved these on monuments set up conscientiously on ceremonial occasions. The old gods were still worshiped, and their faces and names were carved on the glyphs.

But the northern movement continued. Most of the cities of this Middle Period do not record Mayan dates beyond 10.8.0.0.0. Mayan centers in the extreme northern part of the Yucatán Peninsula, some of which already had small populations in earlier times, now swelled to the proportions of major cities. None of these, of course, were cities in the usual sense. The people who made the stone pyramids and the temples on their summits never lived in these ceremonial centers. The common people lived round about in unpretentious huts close to their small farms much as their descendants do today. They built formalized clusters of pyramids and buildings to the glory of their gods—edifices which are the wonder of all students of antiquity everywhere.

The ceremonial centers of northern Yucatán are usually called the New Empire. The dates recorded in the New Empire cities are the latest of all. Especially troubling to archaeologists was the Mayan practice of recording dates in "short count" at this time. Today we use a kind of short count or abbreviation of the year when we write '60 for 1960. We know when we write this date that we mean 1960, but archaeologists five hundred years hence might not know whether we meant 1860, 1960, or 2060. The Mayan abbreviations confused modern archaeologists in much the same way.

But even with the confusion caused by the "short count," the major outlines of Mayan history are fairly clear. In spite of the name "New Empire" applied to these groups of ceremonial centers, they never were empires in the true political sense, although groups of Mayas did band together in leagues which fought against one another. Also during these late years, there was a moral degeneration. Perhaps it was a moral or religious decline which had plagued the Mayas from the first. Drought probably contributed to their troubles. Even before the Spanish conquerors came, many of the New Empire cities were already abandoned. Some of the others were partly falling into ruins. Perhaps the Mayan story was the same as that of many other great civilizations. With constant civil war they had no chance for material progress. The notation of the "short count" was an indication that even the mathematical calculations were falling into disuse. When the Spanish conquerors came, the Mayan civilization was already falling into decay.

The Montejos conquered an already disorganized and declining people. The final obliteration was the work of the Christian priests who, in their religious zeal, wiped out the last vestiges of the accomplishments of this advanced civilization. However, the good Bishop Landa himself amply attested to the magnitude of these accomplishments in his grudging notations of their existence. Archaeologists are still digging out further clues which tell of the greatness of the Mayas. Perhaps some future scholars will be able to decipher the Mayan glyphs which yet remain unknown. Perhaps from these we will learn of their history or the reason for the abandonment of the Old Empire ceremonial centers. But even if we never learn these pieces of forgotten history, the mathematical calculations of the Mayas alone place them among the most accomplished people of the ancient world.

13

Skulls and Pyramids

FOUR PRIESTS, their bodies covered with black paint, held the arms and legs of a prostrate man. The victim was spread-eagled on his back over a circular stone altar. His body was decorated with a headdress of yellow and green feathers and a cloak of colored plumes. His breast was bare. Above him stood a fifth priest, also beautifully dressed in feather headdress, cloak, and breechcloth with a long obsidian knife in his upraised hand. The priest muttered invocations, then suddenly plunged the obsidian knife downward. With a deft stroke he cut between the ribs of the victim. He scooped out the heart while it was still beating convulsively. He held it in his open bloodstained palm and offered it to the sun, which stood at the zenith. At this, a shout rose from the thousands of people gathered around the foot of the stone pyramid on the summit of which the sacrificial altar stood. At a given signal, the four priests who had been holding the victim tumbled the lifeless body down the steep steps which ascended the west side of the pyramid. The people waiting below took the body and quickly cut it into small pieces. Up above, the four black-painted priests were already taking another victim from a small wooden cage and spreading him on his back across the stone altar.

Thus did the ancient Aztecs appease their gods with human sacrifice. A human life is the greatest gift that men can give to any gods. The human sacrifice rites which were enacted thousands of times on top of the stone pyramids of ancient Mexico were not acts of primitive and barbaric cruelty but manifestations of a complex civilization which had been developing for centuries. This civilization had been long in the making.

The Valley of Mexico is an oval volcanic basin which lies on a high plateau. In ancient times a shallow lake lay at the center of the valley. This valley was a favored spot where Ice Age animals roamed. Ice Age Americans killed these animals for meat. It was at Tepexpan in the Valley of Mexico that a human skeleton was found close to the embedded remains of mammoth, and in other parts of the valley the spear points and stone tools of late Ice Age men have been discovered.

In the Valley of Mexico, also, in post-glacial times later groups learned the secret of agriculture. They planted corn and beans and squash. The volcanic soil and the climate were ideal. Round about Lake Texcoco, named after a tribe which lived there, a number of agricultural communities grew up. With a sure food supply and the sedentary advantages of an agricultural life, these communities flourished. Almost certainly, the secret of agriculture was derived from the south from Central America or the northern portion of South America. The northward spread of the agricultural way of life was especially favored in the Valley of Mexico.

In 1519 A.D. Hernando Cortes marched into this same valley at the head of four hundred Spanish soldiers. He found that civilization there was comparable with that of his native Europe. The valley was dotted with towns so that a Spanish soldier could see a dozen at once. In the middle of the lake, they saw a magnificent city. Across the shimmering water they could see a hundred pyramids with buildings on their summits. There were the square outlines of palace roofs, terraces, and theater areas. Even the hardened Spanish adventurers were awed by the sight. Accustomed as they were to the splendors of Europe, they thought that this Mexican capital built on an island in Lake Texcoco rivaled in magnificence the greatest Spanish city of their day.

Some of the wonders of ancient Mexico have been revealed by the spades of archaeologists. Antiquarians have discovered how the Aztec civilization came to be. But an account of the life of the Mexicans at the height of their glory has been provided for us by a person who saw the customs, spoke with the people, knew their names, and could tell of the pomp and circumstance of the happenings.

Bernal Díaz del Castillo was one of the soldiers of Cortes. When Bernal Díaz took part in the great march into the Aztec treasure city, he served as a regular soldier and by all accounts he was a very good one. Years later, when Bernal Díaz was an old man, he wrote a book, ostensibly to correct some wild rumors and misconceptions about this epic adventure into the Valley of Mexico. Díaz called his book *The True History of the Conquest of New Spain.* In this writing, Bernal Díaz became a sort of war correspondent for Cortes. He tells of the military campaigns which destroyed the Mexican empire. Quite unconsciously,

Bernal Díaz paints a vivid picture of a great American culture at the height of its glory. As such, it provides archaeological data of the most revealing sort.

The Aztecs whom Bernal Díaz described with their stone pyramids, their gaily dressed priests, and their human sacrifices, were people who had been through a long period of development. The ceremonies, the sacrifices which solemnized the ceremonies, and the calendar upon which the ceremonies were based were not originated by the Aztecs. Even the methods of building flat-topped pyramids and the other masonry structures of the Aztec capital had been learned from earlier enlightened people.

Agriculture, the key to the entire process of civilization, had certainly begun to the south. Unfortunately, the New World Indians had never discovered the domestication of animals. Outside of a few monkeys, and birds kept for their colored feathers, the Central American peoples never learned that the husbanding of animals would lighten their load and increase their food supply. Of course, as far as the Mexicans and Mayas were concerned, there were few animals in their terrain that were appropriate for domestication. In the Old World, the beginning of civilization was based upon agriculture and the use of domestic animals. In ancient America it was agriculture alone.

The Valley of Mexico was at first a northern outpost of many agricultural communities. Archaeologists have found evidences of a very early people in the valley who had planted corn, beans, and squash and made some pottery. These people they called the "Archaic." Some of the evidences of the Archaic people in the Valley of Mexico go back many centuries before the birth of Christ. It is possible that agriculture itself may have begun as early as 3000 B.C. Because the Valley of Mexico was so well endowed by nature for the agricultural way of life, the people there flourished and the population increased.

But those elements which go to make up greatness were not at first present in the valley around Lake Texcoco. Or perhaps the Mayas and the Central Americans farther south had a head start in these things. The higher civilization of Mexico was based upon the calendar, the building of stone pyramids, and the ceremonial rituals that went with the calendar and the pyramids. These came from the south.

The introduction of these advanced ideas to the Valley of Mexico is often attributed to a mysterious people called the Toltecs. There is some doubt as to whether the Toltecs were a tribe, a group of tribes, or whether the name can only be used to designate a period. It is certain, however, that agricultural people moving north through what is now southern Mexico brought these ideas into the valley. Later on, groups of tribes began to practice ceremonies and build stone pyramids in imitation of their southern neighbors, and there is no doubt that ceremonial cities of stone pyramids in the Valley of Mexico were built much later than those in the Mayan area. It was certainly after the time of Christ that pyramid building and the calendar reached their peak in the Valley of Mexico. Once started there, these ceremonial ingredients produced a civilization unparalleled in ancient America.

The great site of San Juan Teotihuacán lies some 25 miles north of the present city of Mexico. When Cortes and his army marched into the valley in 1519, they must have passed close to the spot and yet no mention was made of it, for the ceremonial city of Teotihuacán was already dead and largely forgotten by Aztec times.

Teotihuacán is nonetheless the most impressive ceremonial center of ancient America. Although not as large as Tikal or some of the Mayan cities, it is of grandiose size and contains the largest extant structures of the civilizations of pre-European times.

The main ceremonial center of Teotihuacán is a vast area three by five miles in extent. At its center is a long plaza or road about one mile long. Along both sides of this "Avenida de las Muertas," or street of the dead, as it is called today, stone pyramids are arranged in a somewhat balanced plan. The general layout of Teotihuacán is similar to that of the Mayan cities and undoubtedly derived from the same source. If the original builders of Teotihuacán intended to balance the many buildings in a perfect plan, they never finished their ambitious scheme. The two major pyramids lie at one end of the long plaza. Most of the others are placed along the eastern side. Many of the pyramids are small. Some of those on the outskirts were built of adobe faced with stone or made of earth entirely. One interesting feature is that many of the pyramids were not erected all at once. Thus, a small pyramid was enlarged by building a larger structure completely over it. Later, a still larger structure was built over the second. Many of the pyramids at Teotihuacán show seven or more enlargements. Just as we are certain that the calendar was already used by these ancient builders, we are equally certain that these pyramid accretions were added every 52 years.

In all, there are about 300 pyramids in the great complex of Teotihuacán. Most of these have been enlarged two or more times. Most are stone-faced or built of stone, and the majority have steep flights of stairs leading to their summits. The pyramid faces were covered with plaster stucco and painted red. These pyramids are much like the Mayan in appearance and function. However, at Teotihuacán there are no stone temples built on the pyramid summits. There probably were structures on the top of the Teotihuacán pyramids, but these must have been built of wood and have long since vanished.

At first glance the ceremonial center of Teotihuacán looks more plain and austere than the Mayan cities. The Mexican pyramids lack the ornate masks and intricate architectural patterns of the Mayan buildings, but two of the pyramids at Teotihuacán are far bigger than anything the Mayan builders accomplished.

These two pyramids are called by the excavators the Pyramid of the Sun and the Pyramid of the Moon, and they may have had something to do with these ancient deities. The Pyramid of the Sun is the largest, with a height of over 200 feet and basal dimensions of over 700 feet on each side. The Pyramid of the Sun at Teotihuacán is only slightly smaller than the famous pyramid of Cheops near Cairo in Egypt. By boring tunnels into the heart of the Pyramid of the Sun archaeologists have discovered that it also was composed of a number of pyramids, each built over the shell of a former one. The cut lava blocks of stone of which the pyramid was built were shaped carefully and laid in even ashlars in a way which would be a credit to any modern builder.

Farther down the Avenida de las Muertas is another great complex of pyramids, the "Ciudadela." This looks like a citadel or fortress but was undoubtedly nothing of the sort. It was a ceremonial building like all the rest at Teotihuacán. The Ciudadela consists of a large platform of stone with a sunken center or courtyard. Within the courtyard is a pyramid of modest dimensions but with terraces and stairways ornately decorated with carvings in hard lava rock. As most of the pyramids at Teotihuacán are plain to the point of being austere, this one is outstanding. The major pyramid of the Ciudadela was probably dedicated to the Mexican god Quetzalcoatl or "Feathered

Serpent." The terraces of the pyramid are decorated with the undulating bodies of serpents. The heads of these serpents protrude to flank the central stairway in a balustrade on either side. Around the necks of these grotesque heads are ruffs of feathers. The whole forms a bold and grotesque façade. The Temple of Quetzalcoatl demonstrates that the builders of Teotihuacán, whoever they were, were true artists and could carve hard stone with great skill.

Even the Pyramid of the Sun at Teotihuacán is not the largest structure in the Mexican complex. At the ancient site of Cholula, some 90 miles away, is another even larger pyramid which stands at the center of about 100 other pyramid mounds in the Cholula Valley. The pyramid of Cholula, near the modern city of the same name, is often ignored by tourists because the outer shell of stone has been stripped away and the remaining structure appears to be entirely of earth. The Christian conquerors built a cathedral on top of the pyramid so that its sanctity could exorcise the evil gods whose rites had formerly been practiced on that summit. At present, the Cholula pyramid looks like a gigantic hill with a church on its top.

The Cholula pyramid is the largest artificial structure in the world and is far more impressive than any in ancient America. In height it is slightly less than 200 feet and its base measures 1,500 feet on each side. The whole pyramid covers about 60 acres. As one might expect, when the archaeologists dug tunnels into the heart of the pyramid, they found several earlier structures built of cut stone. One of the earlier pyramids was circular.

Bernal Díaz made no mention of Teotihuacán but he did describe Cholula, saying that there were over 100 "towers" there, each one placed in a spacious court, with one tower larger than all the rest. Díaz thought Cholula looked like Valladolid in Spain, which was a supreme compliment from the grim old soldier.

This fervor for pyramid building which came out of the south reached its apex among several peoples in and around the Valley of Mexico. With the pyramids came the calendar. When Cortes invaded the Valley of Mexico, the calendar had already been in use there for several centuries.

The Mexican calendar has the same basic elements as the Mayan. Twenty named days grouped into 18 named months made up a 360-day solar year. At the end was a period of 5 unlucky days when nothing could be accomplished and no new projects started. Such names of days as crocodile and monkey indicate plainly the southern origin of the calendar, as there are neither crocodiles nor monkeys in the Valley of Mexico. In addition to the solar year, the Mexicans observed the *tonalamatl* or ceremonial year of 260 days. They also meticulously observed a 584-day year based on the movements of the planet Venus. Five Venus years equaled 8 solar years of 2,920 days.

The number 13 appears in the Mexican calendar as in the Mayan. The 13 numbers were combined with the 20 name days in a continuous sequence. Four of the 20 days of the Mexican calendar could begin a new year. These days were called "year bearers" by the Mexicans and were named house, rabbit, cane, and flint. The Mexican calendar proceeded with one of the 13 numbers attached to each of the year bearers. Thus, the first year of a cycle would be called the year 1 house, the second year would be designated as the year 1 rabbit, the third 1 cane, and so on. A cycle was completed, as the Mexicans expressed it, when each of the year bearers had reigned 13 times. Four times 13 equals 52. Every 52 years the Mexican calendar started all over again.

It is interesting to note that the Mexican mathematicians

did not use the bar and dot system of the Mayas. Nor did they calculate a calendar with periods larger than 52 years. Mexican mathematical calculations were rudimentary compared with the Mayan ones. The Mexicans also did not realize the usefulness of the sign for zero.

The arrival of the Spanish army in 1519 corresponded to the year 2 flint in Mexican chronology. There is no doubt as to the correlation of the Mexican calendar with our own. However, the earlier 52-year periods are extremely vague, especially since the earlier Mexicans seldom recorded dates on stones. When studying earlier times, it is often impossible for archaeologists to determine which 52-year period was meant.

With the building of pyramids and the keeping of the calendar came also the ceremonies which were enacted on top of the pyramids on certain fixed dates. At the end of each 52-year cycle and the beginning of a new one, the Mexicans celebrated a colossal new year throughout the land. Debts were canceled, hostilities were ended, all agreements terminated. Every housewife threw out all her cooking utensils and furniture and began with new ones. Every fire was extinguished. As the day dawned to begin a new 52-year cycle, a fire was kindled on the breast of a slave who was sacrificed for the purpose. From this one fire, torches were carried to every town to light the fires of the new cycle. Thus was the evil of the old 52-year period blotted out and everything begun afresh.

The Mexican gods whose rites were solemnized on the pyramids at calendric periods were also similar to the Mayan. The feathered serpent, or deity of earth and sky, was the major one of these. There were water gods, sky gods, wind gods, and gods of the growing corn in the various seasons. Each of the 20 days and each of the 13 numbers had its own deity.

Most of our information about the Mexican calendar and ceremonials comes from a number of codices or Mexican books. Fortunately the Christians in Mexico were not as successful in destroying all of the Mexican literature as the religious zealots had been in the Mayan area. Several dozen Mexican books have survived from these early times. Some of them were written before the coming of the Spaniards and some were inscribed in post-Spanish times. From these codices, archaeologists have gained a remarkable insight into the ceremonial life of the ancient Mexicans.

Some of the books deal with history. One such is called the Codex Boturini. This is a long scroll on which is told the story of the mysterious Toltecs. Unfortunately, because of the 52-year-cycle calendar and the mixing of much mythological information, it is uncertain history at best. Other codices deal with the history of families with descriptions of daily life, petitions, tributes, rituals, and ceremonies. Most of the codices are calendars arranged into an almanac. It would seem that the subject which interested the Mexican priests most was astrology. A pre-Columbian book called the Codex Vaticanus, because it turned up in the Vatican library, shows an arrangement of the 20 days of the calendar and the 13 numbers. Each of these is ruled over by a guardian deity. Some Spanish soldier, who probably acquired the codex as a souvenir, had placed on each of these days the letters B, M, or I. This Spanish soldier had been told by a Mexican priest which of the days was *bueno, malo,* or *indiferente.*

For the Mexican of centuries ago, these books were used as a means for foretelling the future. A priest with such an almanac would be able to tell a parishioner if the day chosen for a coming marriage or battle was propitious or not.

Many of the Mexican codices would not now be known if it had not been for the work of an English gentlemen of the last century called Lord Kingsborough. Kingsborough was fired with enthusiasm when, as a student at Oxford, he saw some ancient Mexican codices which had found their way into the Bodleian Library. Kingsborough spent his life, which was tragically short, collecting other Mexican manuscripts, one of which bears his name, the Kingsborough Codex. Lord Kingsborough especially wanted to prove by these ancient books that the Mexicans were descendants of the Ten Lost Tribes of Israel. Kingsborough published a magnificent series of the Mexican codices complete with hand-colored illustrations. This he called *Antiquities of Mexico*. The publication cost him his life, for he died ignominiously in a debtors' prison in Dublin, Ireland, as a result of debts contracted in the publication of the book.

The Mexicans also had a series of glyphs. These glyphs bear little resemblance to the Mayan and are generally pictorial. The Mexicans were concerned in their glyphic writing with such things as conquered towns, the paying of tribute, and ceremonial affairs. Some of the Mexican glyphs came close to forming an alphabet system. However, the glyphic writing of the Mexican codices expresses only the most rudimentary ideas. Fortunately this glyphic writing was still in existence at the time of the Spanish conquest. Even Christian prayers taught to the Indians by enthusiastic friars were at first written in Mexican glyphs.

The Mexicans did not carve carefully calculated dates on stone pillars as the Mayas did, but decorated their monuments with grotesque designs which had to do with sacred ceremonies. They seldom recorded dates. Prominent among the Mexican designs were human skulls and human bones. Severed hands, human fingers, human hearts, and other macabre representations are typical of Mexican art. Often the gaily robed and befeathered priests who were the officials of the rituals are shown with these death motifs. Chief among Mexican rituals were offerings made to various gods. It is logical to make an offering to a god if you are asking a favor. If the rain gods were to send rain from the heavens, they were offered gold or jade or feathered plumes. The most valuable thing which can be offered is human life. The Mayas were accustomed to practice human sacrifice on many occasions. Among the Mexicans, human sacrifice became an obsession.

Bernal Díaz, describes the human sacrifices of the Aztecs in vivid terms. Some of his own companions had been dragged off and placed in cages until they were fat enough to serve as a sacrifice at some Mexican festival. Las Casas, an early Spanish priest historian, states that in the last days of their power, the Aztecs were sacrificing 20,000 prisoners yearly and cut out the hearts of 400 victims to celebrate the founding of a single temple. The chief purpose of the warfare which the later Mexicans engaged in so enthusiastically was to capture prisoners to be used for human sacrifice. Pictures of pyramids drawn or painted by Spaniards who witnessed Mexican ceremonies always show the steps covered with the blood of the sacrificial victims whose lifeless bodies were thrown down to be cut up by the waiting populace below. Apparently, on most of these occasions, the Mexican people cut up these bodies and ate the pieces. This was a form of ceremonial cannibalism. If the heart of the victim was offered to the sun, then his body partook of the sanctity of the sun.

One form of human sacrifice which the Mexicans practiced was to dress the potential victim in full regalia and arm him with a club made of feathers. He was then tied by one ankle with a rope of short length attached to the top of a large stone on the summit of a pyramid. Against him was pitted a Mexican warrior with a shield and a wooden club edged with keen obsidian blades. The populace must have enjoyed very much seeing how long the hapless victim on his short tether could avoid the slash of the knife club which would inevitably end his life.

All of these elements of Mexican culture were already present in the Valley of Mexico before the Aztecs ever arrived. By 1000 A.D. several groups of peoples lived around Lake Texcoco in the middle of the valley. All of these had the 52-year calendar, built pyramids, and practised sacrifice and other rituals. About the twelfth century the Aztecs moved in. According to their own traditional account, the Aztecs were a wild untutored tribe who originally came from an island in a salt lagoon. If there is any truth in this account, they originally came from the coast, probably from the northeast. The traditional history goes on to say that the Aztecs started the migration, carrying with them only their major god, Huitzilipochtli, the hummingbird god. According to a prophecy, they were to settle at that spot on which they would find an eagle sitting on a stone in the midst of a cactus. In the beak of the eagle should be a serpent. After years of wandering, they came into the Valley of Mexico. There on the edge of the lake was an eagle sitting on a stone surrounded by cactus and holding a snake in its beak. This symbol is now on the seal of Mexico and appears on the Mexican national flag.

The Aztecs' difficulties did not end with their discovery of the promised land. Like the Israelites of old, they found other people already there. But they managed to settle in this place anyway, possibly partly because the tribes already inhabiting the Valley of Mexico, in spite of their higher culture, were fighting among themselves.

The Aztecs began to build their city on a marshy island in the middle of the lake. They soon learned the cutting of stone and the building of pyramids from their neighbors. Within a few years they had learned to observe the calendar and at the end of the 52-year periods they too rebuilt their pyramids. In the matter of human sacrifice, the newly initiated Aztecs became more enthusiastic than their teachers. Thus this people soon took over a culture which they had not made. It was the Aztecs who brought Mexican civilization to its zenith. They called their city in the middle of the lake Tenochtitlán, "place where the god in cactus sits on a stone." The marshy island was strengthened by stone platforms and plazas. Three great causeways connected the island city with the mainland. The causeways were interrupted periodically by drawbridges for defense. In the midst of the city they built palaces, places for rituals and dancing, and even a special building for the keeping of birds so that they might have a plentiful supply of colored feathers. But greatest of all were the stone pyramids which they erected to the glory of their gods, especially to Huitzilipochtli, their patron deity. When this civilization was at its height, there were undoubtedly hundreds of stone pyramids rising above the housetops of Tenochtitlán. The great pyramid or *teocalli,* which means "house of the god," was the most important structure of its kind in all of Mexico. We can only presume that the great teocalli of Tenochtitlán was far more impressive than that at either Teotihuacán or Cholula.

It is small wonder that the Spanish soldiers, when they first saw the city of Tenochtitlán across the waters of Lake Texcoco were amazed at its size and magnificence. Even Cortes and his followers were impressed by the many stone buildings, palaces, and courtyards they found there. They likened Tenochtitlán to Venice because of its many canals.

Certainly at the time when Cortes and his Spanish army fought in its streets, Tenochtitlán was the most magnificent and impressive city in all of North and South America. Not even any Mayan center was so large or well built as the capital of the Aztecs.

The Spaniards stole the treasure of Montezuma. They were forced out of the city, fighting as they went. Then Cortes came back with another army and Indian allies. The city of Tenochtitlán fell and its treasure was taken. In a later campaign to the south, Cortes carried with him Cuatemoc, the last ruler of the Aztecs. In the blackest deed of treachery of his bloody career, Cortes murdered Cuatemoc and so ended the Mexican royal line forever. Actually, the brilliant culture of the Valley of Mexico was doomed when the first Spaniard crossed the causeway and entered the city of Tenochtitlán.

Just as in the Mayan area, it was Christian enthusiasts who completed the destruction which the Spanish soldiers had started. Not only were the remaining Aztecs swiftly converted to Christianity, but all pagan monuments were summarily destroyed. The main teocalli was pulled down, stone by stone. A Christian cathedral, now the great cathedral of Mexico, was built in its place. The high altar of this cathedral was thought the best means of holding down the evil spirits lingering in this place of infamy as a result of the thousands of human sacrifices that had been made there. All the other pyramids were destroyed. The building materials were used for modern buildings or for paving streets or filling in the shallows of Lake Texcoco, Modern Mexico City rose on the leveled ruin of what had once been magnificent Tenochtitlán. The Zocalo, the great open square in the midst of Mexico City, now occupies the same position as the main plaza which the Aztecs had built there. Here and there, below modern street level, a visitor may occasionally find the stub of a pyramid, or the fragment of a stone wall, or a carved stone serpent which mark the sites of some of the Aztec edifices. But little else remains of the great city, the largest and most magnificent of ancient America.

But there are other ceremonial centers in many spots in central and southern Mexico. Several peoples, the Totonacs, the Olmecs, the Zapotecs, and others, had learned to build stone pyramids and observe a calendar of the seasons and rituals to go with them. In the years to come, archaeologists will be able to fill in the gaps in the history of the pyramid builders and calendar keepers of Mexico and Central America.

14

The Andean Incas

ATAHUALPA stood in the middle of the town square of Caxamarca. Flickering light from the many torches carried by the Spanish soldiers played upon the handsome features and muscular body of the monarch. His face looked composed as the Spanish executioners bound him to a post in the middle of the square and piled bundles of wooden faggots around him. Father Vincente de Valverde moved to the side of the condemned man. The friar, who had that very evening made the statement that Atahualpa deserved death, now tried to persuade the doomed king to forswear the religion of his ancestors and embrace Christianity. As a further inducement, Father Valverde promised that instead of being burned at the stake, Atahualpa would be killed by the "garrote," which is the strangling cord reserved for Spanish criminals. Atahualpa turned his face toward the Spanish leader Pizarro. It was Pizarro who had promised

Atahualpa freedom if he filled the room of his captivity in Caxamarca with gold, and the room next to it twice over with silver. Atahualpa had sent his subjects to all parts of the kingdom. They had brought the gold and the silver, stripping the plates of metal from the walls of their temples to do so. Now Pizarro, with black treachery, was meting out death as his part of the bargain. A minute before the faggots were lighted, Atahualpa renounced the gods of his fathers and embraced the cross. Father Valverde gave him the Christian name of Juan de Atahualpa. From behind, a soldier tightened the garrote. Juan de Atahualpa slumped downward in his chains. So died the last Inca, the son of the sun, the last ruler of a mighty kingdom in the Andes.

When Atahualpa was perfidiously murdered by Pizarro and his soldiers, it was just after sunset on the 29th of August, 1533. Thirteen years before, Cortes had brought an end to the great Mexican civilization when he sacked the Mexican capital of Tenochtitlán. Later, Cortes treacherously murdered Cuatemoc, the successor to Montezuma and the last legitimate ruler of the Aztecs. Pizarro had a precedent in the destruction of a whole civilization and the murder of its last king. By this murder Pizarro also brought an end to an American kingdom.

Atahualpa was the ruler of the Incan Empire. He had been the absolute monarch of all the area and people extending from modern Ecuador south to northern Chile and inland to the headwaters of the Amazon. Within this great area were terraced cities and stone buildings, mighty fortresses, towers, barracks, and bridges. In places, flat-topped and terraced pyramids had been erected as religious structures. In some material accomplishments these Andean civilizations were more outstanding than any others in ancient America. But just as the Aztecs of the Valley of Mexico had learned all of their lore from earlier peoples, so also had the Incas of the Andes. The Incas had received their empire from earlier peoples who had developed the architecture, the religion, and the art which Pizarro found.

Archaeologically, the Andean area is really two areas. Along the coast of Ecuador, Peru, and northern Chile is a strip of dry desert country extending from the foot of the mountains to the sea. This area is, in most places, almost waterless except where the numerous river valleys carry water to the coast from their tributaries in the Andes. The coastal Andean area is divided into a number of river valley segments. Ancient people lived in these river valleys. They irrigated their farms with the mountain water which flowed down in rivers. They built their religious pyramids and placed their cemeteries in the desert which bordered the coast.

In the Andes Mountains themselves, and especially in their valleys, are many sites which comprised another ancient region. The people in the mountain areas had different ways of life and different sorts of buildings from those on the coast. The mountain Andeans and the coastal Andeans knew and communicated with each other, but they followed separate ways during the course of much of their civilization. Archaeologists now recognize several kinds of ancient coastal Andeans and separate varieties of mountain civilizations.

It is remarkable that any great civilizations ever began or flourished in the Andean area at all. The coastal region is desert-like and inhospitable. The cordilleras of the Andes themselves are precipitous and barren. Many of the valleys are extremely high, and cold mountain fogs and drizzling rain are usual conditions. We rather expect great civilizations to start in favorable river valleys where soil and climate make it easy for men to produce food.

Some men had found their way into South America at

a very early date. Dr. Junius Bird of the American Museum of Natural History, digging in the extreme southern tip of Chile in the late 1930s, found camp sites and caves where ancient people had lived. Radioactive carbon dates later derived from charred sloth and horse bones from these caves prove that human beings lived there at least 6,000 years before Christ. The inhabitants of these caves had been hunters and food gatherers. They hunted mostly the guanaco, a variety of camel which still lives in the southern portion of South America, and the now extinct Ice Age horse. Presumably, these early people had found their way down through the Isthmus of Panama from North America and thence by devious routes to the southern portion of South America where Dr. Bird found the ashes of their campfires. Some of them may have gone south through the jungles of the Amazon Basin. A better guess is that groups of these early migrants moved south by way of the Andean valleys or along the coast of Peru. In the Andean area, they found spots to their liking. Some of them stayed there. Certainly the Andean life began a very long time ago.

Camp sites along the coast show that some of these early dwellers lived there by gathering shellfish and wild vegetable foods. There were early dwellers in the Andean valleys also. In the mountains, they hunted wild camels which remained from Ice Age times and perhaps developed the first agricultural products. It is doubtful whether maize itself was first grown in the Andes, but certainly the white potato and certain kinds of beans are native to the area.

Agricultural life may have begun earlier in Peru and Ecuador than in any other place in America. Radioactive carbon tests show that agriculture was practiced on the Peruvian coast at least 4,500 years ago. The first products they raised in their primitive fields were peanuts, cotton, and gourds, but no maize. Even from these earliest times, the archaeological history of the Andean area is twofold. Groups of farmers, using irrigation ditches, raised their garden produce in the valleys along the coastal strip. At the same time, in the mountain areas, other Andean farmers evolved cultures of a different sort. The coastal people and the mountain people were, during most of the prehistoric life of the Andean area, distinct.

When the Spaniards conquered the Incan Empire, Peru became known as the land of beautiful pottery. By the end of the sixteenth century, European merchants were bringing from Peru exquisitely made vessels with bizarre designs painted in many colors. These characteristic and brilliantly ornamented pottery pieces began to turn up in collections and museums long before anyone knew who had made them or where they fitted into Andean archaeology. Usually these beautiful pieces of Peruvian pottery were simply dubbed "Incan," with no other information given. As soon as archaeologists began to dig in Peru, it became evident that these polychrome pottery vessels were not Incan at all. They had been made by a people who lived on the coasts and in the mountains of Peru many centuries before the existence of the Incan Empire.

Soon after agriculture appeared in the Andean area, each farming community in the river valleys and mountain areas produced a distinct kind of pottery. The most famous, however, and certainly that most coveted by collectors, was a beautiful variety which came from the Nazca Valley in southern Peru. Nazca pottery, of which several varieties are now recognized, is one of the most beautiful ceramic products of ancient America, and perhaps of the whole world.

Attracted by the pottery, a number of archaeologists in the 1920s explored the Nazca Valley and began to excavate.

But by the time the first archaeologists began to dig in Nazca, over 50,000 pieces of Nazca pottery had already been dug by the local inhabitants and sold as curios. Most of the ancient tombs where the pottery had been placed by the original inhabitants had been ravaged and destroyed by native diggers. The archaeologists were also disappointed to find little surface evidence of a great civilization in the Nazca Valley. There were a few "huacas" or adobe flat-topped pyramids of modest size. They found some house remains outlined by hand-made adobe bricks, and some of the hillsides along the Nazca Valley were artificially terraced. But none of these evidences of architecture compared in size or workmanship with the architecture of the Mayas, who had built stone pyramids and stone temples with such skill. Indeed, there were other ancient people in Peru itself who surpassed the Nazcas in the trappings of civilization. The archaeologists gained the impression that the Nazca Valley was at the southernmost extension of the pyramid-building and architectural development of early America.

In another respect, too, the archaeologists were disappointed in Nazca. From a number of ancient sites in Peru and Ecuador, early diggers had procured objects of copper, bronze, gold, and silver. It was the abundance of gold which had lured the greedy Spaniards to the Incan Empire in the first place. But in the few Nazca tombs which the archaeologists found undisturbed, they uncovered little metal. The ancient Nazcas had pounded out some gold nuggets into narrow strips of beaten gold. These they decorated with repoussé designs showing masks of the faces of demons. Generally the Nazcas had little gold, a very little copper, and no silver at all.

But in two particulars the Nazcas were supreme. They made exquisite pottery and they wove textiles which were the most advanced in ancient America. Nazca pottery is now recognized by every archaeologist. The shapes of the vessels and the delicacy of their manufacture show an advanced ceramic technique, greater than that achieved by the Mayas or the Mexicans, or for that matter by any of the North American civilized people. The Nazca potters specialized in exotic polychrome shades embodying such colors as purple, magenta, blue, black, and a number of others not achieved by other early potters. Apparently these beautifully colored vessels were manufactured, for the most part, to place in tombs with the dead.

The Nazca farmers had prepared resting places for their honored dead, usually in the desert along the edges of the valley. They dug a pit some ten or twelve feet deep and lined the bottom with carefully made adobe bricks. The body was placed in this shaft grave in a seated position and accompanied by a dozen or more pottery vessels, undoubtedly containg food and drink for the long hereafter. The body itself was swathed in several layers of clothing. After the burial, the shaft was closed by a layer of poles and rocks, and in some cases an additional adobe capping was placed on top. The remarkable fact about the Nazca burials from the archaeological point of view is that the coastal desert is so dry that in many cases the layers of clothing in which the bodies were wrapped were preserved. If the climate of this area were moist, we probably would know nothing about the Nazca textiles. As it is, archaeologists have recovered thousands of fragments of early Nazca weaving. To study these is to gain a new insight into what the Nazca civilization was.

Some of the Nazca textiles were made of cord manufactured from maguey fiber. Others were of cotton or of wool derived from the wild vicuña or alpaca. Few of the early Nazca textiles were simple in manufacture. Many of them were more complicated than most modern types of cloth. The Nazcas were capable of dyeing and weaving yarns of many colors. A hundred and ninety different hues have been identified by one archaeologist studying Nazca textiles. Such weaves as double cloth, tapestry, gauze, netting, embroidery, and three-dimensional knitting were known and used by the early Nazca weavers. The designs of these complicated techniques in many colors were varied and pleasing. Some of the same designs appear in the textiles and in the pottery. Stylized animals, human figures, masked faces, and geometric lines are common.

With these varied techniques, the Nazca artisans made mantles, tunics, aprons, and cloaks. Especially common were bands, kerchiefs, and veils used as head coverings. Most of their garments were rectangular with very little attempt at shaping or tailoring. Many of the garment types were probably intended especially for the dressing of the dead.

The amazing complexity and advanced techniques in weaving coupled with the refinement of Nazca pottery are abundant indication that the Nazca farmers were not the first to develop these accomplishments. Polychrome-painted and beautifully shaped pottery vessels were undoubtedly developed by earlier peoples. Fine textiles of complicated weaves are also typical of most places in the Andean area. Their beginnings undoubtedly go back to remote antiquity.

Nor were the Nazca farmers the only ones in the coastal area in these early times. Just north of Nazca, the Ica Valley is also an archeologist's paradise for pottery and textiles. From Paracas, north of the Ica Valley, "mummies" have been found in a better state of preservation than anywhere in the Andean area. In the Paracas tombs deep shafts were dug into the desert soil, opening out at the bottom into rooms of considerable size. In these large rooms bodies were buried sitting in a circle and wrapped in multiple layers of beautiful textiles. Some graves at Paracas contained as many as forty-eight swathed and seated mummy figures arranged in a circle. The Paracas textiles outdo even the Nazca fabrics in complexity of manufacture, color, and design.

North of Paracas, where other mountain rivers flow down to the sea, still other ancient farmers made pottery and wove beautiful fabrics. In these northern areas, flat-topped pyramids and other architectural evidences become more plentiful. But none of the coastal cultures developed the cutting of stone on a large scale or used stone for buildings.

While the early farmers of the coastal valley were working out their destinies and lending expression to their artistic feelings in pottery and textiles, other groups of Andeans in the mountain areas were carrying on in their own way. Perhaps the greatest site in the whole Andean area is that at Tiahuanaco, at the southern end of Lake Titicaca in Bolivia. Whereas the coastal peoples had not developed the art of building in stone, the inhabitants of the valley around Lake Titicaca had learned to cut stone and erect monumental buildings.

When first seen by the Spanish conquerors in 1550, the great site of Tiahuanaco was already in ruins. Apparently the main buildings were at one time a vast palace, although it has been suggested that the place was once an observatory for watching the movements of the sun, and some archaeologists believe that Tiahuanaco was actually a lake port. The major remains, outlined by large upright stones beautifully cut and placed, consist of large quadrangles, some 440 by 400 feet, which are laid out due east and west. Most of the structures which were originally built on these quadrangles were apparently made of adobe or smaller stones. Beneath the massive foundations are underground vaults. Indeed, most of the remaining site is underground. The stones of the foundations and the vaults of these grandiose buildings are precisely cut and held together with metal clamps instead of mortar.

One of the outstanding features of the site of Tiahuanaco is the Gateway to the Sun, which probably formed a doorway to part of the building complex. The whole gateway is monolith with six niches carved into the back and four friezes of decoration in high relief on the front. The pictures of running bird men found on the face of the gateway are also present in the textile designs. A system of suns in the decoration has given the gateway its name.

Tiahuanaco is only one of many sites in the Lake Titicaca region. The early inhabitants here had learned to cut stone and fit it together with great skill. Excavations around the site and others in the same region have shown that the inhabitants had an abundance of metal. They had a great deal of copper and some bronze. The clamps which held the building stones together were made of copper. The chisels and tools with which the stones were shaped were made of copper alloys and bronze.

Pottery of the Tiahuanaco people is also distinctive and very different from the Nazca. Tiahuanaco pottery is also decorated in many colors. It is often decorated not only with painting but also with relief carvings of animals such as cats and llamas, figures wearing masks and carrying trophy heads. From the pottery and also the carving on such monuments as the Gateway to the Sun, archaeologists recognize a Tiahuanaco style.

There is little doubt that the builders of the great site of Tiahuanaco were cutting stones and laying them to form the foundations of the great buildings there about

1000 A.D. at the time that the Nazca farmers were digging their irrigation ditches in the valley on the coast. At several periods the mountain dwellers, such as those at Tiahuanaco, moved out of the mountains by means of trade and conquest and influenced the whole region.

To the north, and also in the mountains, lies the mysterious site of Chavin. At Chavin, agricultural people had erected buildings and established a high civilization even earlier than that of Tiahuanaco—perhaps as early as 800 years before Christ. The main site consists of a sequence of mounds reminiscent of the great ceremonial centers of the Mayas. In the center of this group are two superimposed platforms surrounded by a complex of outbuildings. The great temple of Chavin is on top of a platform and is built in the form of an ornate pyramid. A cut stone stairway leads to the summit. Inside the great temple and its surrounding platform is a labyrinth of corridors, galleries, and rooms. Niches in the walls undoubtedly once contained idols which have long since disappeared. Only one carving remains in the interior of the main pyramid. This is a granite shaft shaped like a gigantic dagger which extends from the floor to the ceiling of one of the many chambers. The entire surface of the stone dagger is carved with beautiful relief sculpture. The ancient artist carved a deity with a feline head and prominent cat fangs in its mouth and snakes for hair.

In early Andean times, a style of carving and making pottery spread from the great site of Chavin. Other early peoples, even those on the coast, copied the catlike faces with the protruding fangs of the Chavin carvers. Chavinoid pottery also featured feline heads and teeth, usually carved in relief. We can only suppose that merchants and, in some cases, armies marched down out of the highlands and took over the coastal valleys. Archaeologists, with the clues of stylistic motifs, textile designs, and pottery types can follow these ancient movements even though the names of the important individuals and the specific events of these early fragments of American history have been forgotten for many centuries.

The many coastal cultures and the several developments in the highlands were amalgamated in later times by a series of political happenings which resulted in the formation of a true empire. Again, archaeologists can follow the trend of events only in major outline. The most important people of this time of amalgamation were the farmers of the Chimu Valley on the coast. In very early Andean times, the Chimus had exerted a great influence upon the mountain peoples and upon surrounding areas. Early Chimu pottery is one of the outstanding types known by archaeologists and collectors. After a series of political events which must have involved the marching and countermarching of armies, the Chimus managed to build an empire of sorts which had some political unity. The Chimu Empire borders upon the historic period and probably reached its height somewhere around the thirteenth century A.D. Legendary accounts of later times tell of great Chimu chieftains and of a kingdom which covered most of the coast and the Andean highlands.

As proof that the Chimus were the organizers recounted in these legends is the famous site of Chan Chan, which can only be described as a city. Chan Chan, the capital of the Chimu Empire, is one of the very few ancient sites which compares with a modern large city. The remains of Chan Chan cover eleven square miles and consist of a complex of streets, palaces, and buildings with adobe walls. The whole city was carefully laid out in units or so-called "citadels," each one of which was a separate city in itself. An airplane view of this enormous work of the early Andeans shows that this was a very great civilization. Only highly organized people with a political empire and religious unity could have built a city of such a size and regular plan.

At the height of its power, the Chimu Empire stretched from modern Ecuador far south along the Peruvian coast to include most of the coastal valleys. The Chimus also held sway over most of the mountain areas. Within this vast domain, they built many cities which are smaller counterparts of Chan Chan. Fortresses, flat-topped pyramids, and irrigation systems are products of the organizational ability of the Chimus. Artistically, the late Chimu Empire was perhaps not so fine. Pottery styles lacked the beauty and finish of earlier times. The Chimu adobe architecture is not as thrilling as the cut stone of the early Chavin or Tiahuanaco. Even the flat-topped pyramids are generally of modest size and simple outline. But perhaps the falling off of style was an indication that the Chimus considered the political organization of empire more important than painted pottery or colored textiles. Undoubtedly they also discovered that empire building is a difficult business. There was a period of chaos. The Chimu Empire began to disintegrate into its original elements and peoples. But new organizers had already appeared in the Andean highlands.

When speaking of things Andean, we usually talk glibly of the Inca culture. And yet it becomes apparent from even a cursory examination of Andean antiquity that the Incas were Johnny-come-latelies on the Andean scene. According to tradition, the Incas came from the southern Andean area around Cuzco where the tributaries of the Amazon River flow through deep gorges. Wherever the Incas originally came from, they appeared in the highlands first and learned the culture of the people already there. This was another example of a virile tribe taking on the culture of a preceding people and finally ruling the entire area. Perhaps from the earlier Tiahuanaco builders, the Incas learned the cutting and fitting of large stones. They learned how to make metal tools and weapons from other Andean peoples; and, most important, they learned how to organize many peoples and places into a political empire. There is no doubt that the Incan organization was founded upon the earlier empires.

Cuzco, in the mountains, became the Incan capital. The whole Cuzco valley is full of ancient remains, some of them extremely early. At Cuzco itself is abundant evidence that the Incas took over other civilizations which were already there. Today a visitor to Cuzco can see how well the Incas learned their lessons from earlier peoples. The Sun Temple, the beautifully fitted stone walls of the Cuzco streets, terraces and doorways are evidence of the skill of Inca stone cutters.

Also in the Incan highlands are several great fortress cities, many of them not far from Cuzco. Machu Picchu is typical of these military towns of the Incas. Here again there is archaeological evidence that earlier people had occupied the place in previous centuries. But the terraces and megalithic stone walls that the visitor sees today tell of the greatness of the Incas who pulled together all of these earlier efforts.

The Inca overlords, who considered themselves the sons of the sun, extended their dominion over a much larger area than that of the earlier Chimus. Roads were extended to all parts of this empire which stretched at one time from modern Chile and Argentina north to Ecuador. The Incas laid out and in some places paved over 7,000 miles of roads. Bridges of stone crossed major rivers, suspension bridges were constructed across precipitous gorges, and even pontoon bridges were placed over streams which could not otherwise be crossed. Guard houses and fortresses protected the kingdom's communication system. Regular royal messengers relayed news and decrees over these roads. Well-organized armed guards occupied military barracks at strategic places. It is small wonder that with this closely knit organization the Inca rulers were able to amass the wealth of gold which aroused the avarice of the Spanish conquerors.

But even with the high organization of the Incan Empire, characteristics of other American cultures were absent in theirs. None of the Andeans kept track of time with a highly developed calendar of intricate mathematical counts, as the Central American ancients had. Nor did the Andeans evolve a system of glyphs or true writing. The Andeans had developed a method of carrying messages and of counting by using a contrivance made of a series of strings. This was called a "quipu" and consisted of one major cord from which hung a series of strings. These dangling strings were knotted. Each knot represented a count in a decimal system. Each string represented digits in order. Thus, an army commander could send a messenger with a quipu with the order that the number of soldiers represented by the knotted strings be sent on a specific mission. The quipu could also keep track of taxes or astronomic figures. The strings and knots were also colored. However, the quipu was used as an aid to memory and was not a true system of writing.

Because they had no real writing method or calendar, the Andeans never kept records in books. Occasionally they painted signs on large lima beans, and painted beans were often carried by royal messengers as an indication that the message they carried was genuine.

The artistic and intellectual achievements of the Andeans are the fineness of their metal work, the excellence and size of their cut-stone buildings, and especially their organizational ability. And in many ways the Andean ancients were more matter-of-fact than their neighbors to the north. The greatest accomplishments of the Chimu builders and the later Incas were vast cities, terraced fortresses, and mighty stone walls. Relatively little effort was spent by them on pyramids or purely religious buildings. Perhaps this was because the ruler, the Inca himself, was the son of the sun and the greatest deity of the empire.

When Pizarro and his Spanish army captured Atahualpa, the last reigning Inca, they captured the reigning deity of the vast Andean empire. Perhaps the canny Pizarro realized that by treacherously killing Atahualpa, even after the Inca king had fulfilled his pledge of filling his room of captivity with gold to a level as high as he could reach with his outstretched hand, the Spanish could destroy the life of the empire. Even by modern evaluation, the followers of Atahualpa brought $17,000,000 worth of gold to fulfill their part of the pledge. What other people anywhere in the ancient world could have brought so much wealth together in a single pile? The high degree of organization of the Incas was their own downfall. With the death of their supreme leader, the son of the sun, moral confusion was added to military defeats and the whole organization fell apart. A vast system which had been built up by many people over tens of centuries was destroyed by a single jerk of the strangling cord.

But certainly the modern visitor, seeing the remains of ancient life on the Peruvian coast or the stone-built cities of the Andean highlands, will readily realize that here were some of the greatest civilizations of ancient America. It was the Andean people who contributed many of the most important agricultural products to both ancient and modern times. In pottery, weaving, and cut-stone architecture, they were supreme. The Andean cultures are another indication that prehistoric America contained many great minds and great men.

There are many examples of parallelism in human culture. While the civilizations of Egypt, Mesopotamia, India, and China were developing in the Old World, many corresponding civilizations were evolving in America. The Egyptians built pyramids and developed a calendar. So did the Mayas. The important concept of zero was invented by the early Hindus and by ancient American mathematicians. The early Chinese contributed rice to world agriculture, the early American farmers gave corn. By many such parallels in accomplishment it appears that ancient American culture was as important as that of the Old World. Inasmuch as the American culture began later than that of the Old World, the New World civilizations are all the more remarkable. Recent archaeological digging has emphasized this importance of New World antiquity. Future digging will tell more of the American story. We hope the archaeologists of tomorrow will find the skeleton of a Sandia man, will discover the first beginnings of agriculture, the origin of the Eskimos, or the source of the first Mound Builders. Perhaps the next excavation will reveal the secret of the as yet undecipherable Mayan glyphs or solve the mystery of the Toltecs. We have discovered much of the ancient story. There is still much to be found.

A SUGGESTED LIST
OF FURTHER READINGS
IN AMERICAN ARCHAEOLOGY

A Suggested List of Further Readings in American Archaeology

GENERAL

Martin, Quimby, and Collier. *Indians Before Columbus.* Chicago: University of Chicago Press, 1949.

EARLY ICE AGE AMERICANS

Hibben, Frank C. *The Lost Americans.* New York: Thomas Y. Crowell, 1960.

Sellards, E. H. *Early Man in America.* Austin: University of Texas Press, 1952.

Wormington, H. M. *Ancient Man in North America.* Denver Museum of Natural History Popular Series No. 4, revised. Denver, 1957.

MOUND BUILDERS

Griffin, James B. (ed.). *Archaeology of Eastern United States.* Chicago: University of Chicago Press, 1952.

Shetrone, H. C. *The Moundbuilders.* New York: D. Appleton, 1930.

SOUTHWEST

Kidder, A. V. *An Introduction to the Study of Southwestern Archaeology.* New Haven: Yale University Press, 1924.

Wormington, H. M. *Prehistoric Indians of the Southwest.* Denver Museum of Natural History Popular Series No. 7. Denver, 1956.

PLAINS AND SALVAGE ARCHAEOLOGY

Strong, W. D. *An Introduction to Nebraskan Archaeology.* Smithsonian Miscellaneous Collections Vol. XCIII, No. 10. Washington, D.C., 1935.

Wedel, Waldo R. "Changing Settlement Patterns in the Great Plains," in *Prehistoric Settlement Patterns in the New World.* Edited by Gordon P. Willey. Viking Fund Publications in Anthropology No. 23. New York, 1956.

Wendorf, Fred, Fox, Nancy, Lewis, and Arian L. (eds.). *Pipeline Archaeology.* Santa Fe: Laboratory of Anthropology, 1956.

ESKIMO

Collins, H. B., Jr. "Outline of Eskimo Prehistory," in *Essays in Historical Anthropology of North America.* Smithsonian Miscellaneous Collections, Vol. C. Washington, D.C., 1940.

Jenness, Diamond. *Indians of Canada.* Ottawa, 1932.

Rainey, F. G. *Eskimo Prehistory.* American Museum of Natural History Anthropological Papers, Vol. XXXVII, Pt. 4. New York, 1941.

MEXICO

Díaz del Castillo, Bernal. *The True History of the Conquest of New Spain.* Translated by A. D. Mandslay. London: Hakluyt Society, 1908.

Vaillant, G. C. *The Aztecs of Mexico.* Baltimore: Penguin Books, 1956.

MAYAS

Morley, Sylvanus G. *The Ancient Maya.* Stanford, Calif.: Stanford University Press, 1947.

Weatherwax, Paul. *Indian Corn in Old America.* New York: The Macmillan Co., 1954.

ANDEANS

Bennett, Wendell C. "The Archaeology of the Central Andes," in *Handbook of South American Indians,* Vol. 2. Washington, D.C.: Bureau of American Ethnology, 1946.

Bennett, Wendell C., and Bird, Junius B. *Andean Cultural History.* New York, 1949.

INDEX

INDEX